Do-it-yourself

Small Claims

LAW PACK™
GUIDE

First Edition 1996
Second Edition 1999

Copyright 1996, 1999 Law Pack Publishing Limited
Law Pack Small Claims Guide

Law Pack Publishing Limited
76-89 Alscot Road
London SE1 3AW
www.lawpack.co.uk

Printed in the United Kingdom

ISBN: 1-902646-04-5

Table of contents

How to use this Law Pack Guide

This Law Pack Guide can help you achieve an important legal objective conveniently, efficiently and economically. Nevertheless it is important for you to use this Guide properly if you are to avoid later difficulties.

Step-by-step instructions for using this Guide:

1. Read this Guide carefully. If after thorough examination you decide that your requirements are not met by this Guide, or you do not feel confident about writing your own documents, consult a solicitor.

2. At the end of this Guide there are completed examples of the forms needed to handle your own small claim. Contact your local County Court, listed in the telephone directory, to obtain copies of these forms. See page 65 for a full list.

3. Once obtained, make several copies of the original forms for practice, for future use and for updates. You should also make copies of the completed forms. Create a record-keeping system for both sets of copies.

4. When completing your forms, do not leave any section blank. If any section is inapplicable, write 'not applicable' or 'none'. This shows you have not overlooked this section.

5. Always use pen or type on legal documents; never use pencil.

6. Do not cross out or erase anything you have written on your final forms.

7. You will find a helpful glossary of terms at the end of this Guide. Refer to this glossary if you find unfamiliar terms.

8. Always keep legal documents in a safe place and in a location known to your spouse, family, executor or solicitor.

In this Guide, for 'him' read 'him or her'.

Before you file your small claims case

The Small Claims Track in the County Courts is designed to be user friendly. It encourages people to represent themselves in court for the purposes of pursuing simple claims for comparatively small sums. Judges are used to dealing with members of the public, hearings are less formal than in other courts, and the normal rules of evidence do not apply.

On 26th April 1999 new court rules were introduced to cover both the High and County Courts. A new single set of rules covers both courts. Rule 1 sets out the Overriding Objective:

1.1 (1)   These Rules are a new procedural code with the overriding objective of enabling the court to deal with cases justly.
(2) Dealing with a case justly includes, so far as is practicable —
    (a)   ensuring that the parties are on an equal footing;
    (b)   saving expense;
    (c)   dealing with the case in ways which are proportionate —
        (i)   to the amount of money involved;
        (ii)   to the importance of the case;
        (iii) to the complexity of the issues; and
        (iv)   to the financial position of each party;
    (d)   ensuring that it is dealt with expeditiously and fairly; and
    (e)   allotting to it an appropriate share of the court's resources, while taking into account the need to allot resources to other cases.

All cases are now segregated into one of 3 tracks with different procedures adopted for each track.

1.   Small Claims Track — Claims up to £5,000 (and see below).
2.   Fast Track — Claims for £5,000–£15,000 with trial to be no more than 1 day. (There are limited costs recovery rules and trial is guaranteed to take place within 30 weeks of allocation.)
3.   Multi Track — Complex cases and claims over £15,000.

What is the Small Claims Track?

The Small Claims Track is a simplified procedure within the County Court for dealing with claims for amounts of money under £5,000. Although it is not a separate court, it is often called 'the Small Claims Court'.

The Small Claims track covers the following types of case:

- Any claim which has a financial value of not more than £5,000.

- Any claim for personal injuries which has a financial value of not more than £5,000 where the claim for general damages for personal injuries is not more than £1,000.

- Any claim which includes a claim by a tenant of residential premises against his landlord for repairs or other work to the premises where the estimated cost of the repairs or other work is not more than £1,000 and the financial value of any claim for damages in respect of those repairs or other work is not more than £1,000.

Within the County Court there are two types of judges:

1. *Circuit Judges:* these are the more senior, and normally sit in a formal courtroom wearing wigs and gowns.
2. *District Judges:* these normally sit in a room known as chambers and do not wear wigs and gowns. The parties sit around a table and the procedure is less formal.

Small claims cases are, except in special circumstances, dealt with by a District Judge, not by a Circuit Judge.

Advantages of Small Claims Track

1. You can prepare and present your case without having to pay a solicitor. A solicitor's fee will most likely be more than your claim. Under the Small Claims Track you have a chance of recovering the full amount of your loss with little or no cost. You can use a solicitor to represent you, but in most cases a solicitor is not necessary.

2. Making a small claim is a simple process. This Law Pack Guide contains the instructions and completed examples of forms for making a Small Claim. If you have any doubt, the Consumer Advice Centre or a Citizens' Advice Bureau can be of great help.

3. The normal rules that apply in suing someone, many of which are complicated, do not apply in small claims cases. District Judges are used to dealing with people acting for themselves.

CHAPTER 1

What may you sue for?

Currently, you may not sue for an amount larger than £5,000 using the Small Claims Track in the County Court. All claims under £5,000 are automatically referred to the Small Claims Track. The District Judge does, though, have discretion to refer a matter involving more than £5,000 where it is straightforward and does not involve difficult questions of law or evidence.

If your claim is more than £5,000 and you think it is straightforward, ask the court to have your case dealt with as small claims matter.

If you believe you are entitled to more than the current small claims court limit, you can voluntarily lower your claim so you may use the Small Claims Track. This may be advisable if, for instance, you think you have a claim for £5,200. It may be wiser to sacrifice the additional £200 for a faster recovery without legal fees.

Virtually any type of claim within the monetary limit can be brought as a small claim. The following are some typical small claims matters:

- Debt collection
- Landlord/tenant actions
- Personal injury cases

Highlight

You can use a solicitor to represent you, but in most cases a solicitor is not necessary.

SMALL CLAIMS TRACK – *A Brief Outline*

1. **The Claim Arises**
(i) *Unpaid Invoice/Debt*   (ii) *Breach of Contract*   (iii) *Negligence*   (iv) *Faulty Goods*

▼

2. **Attempts to Settle**
(i) *Demand Letter*   (ii) *Telephone Calls*   (iii) *Arbitration*

▼

3. **Issue of Claim Form** *(Form N1)*

▼

4. **Court Serves Claim Form and Response Pack on Defendant**

▼   ▼   ▼

5. (a) Defendant does nothing | (b) Defendant admits and makes an offer | (c) Defendant defends

▼ | ▼ | ▼

Default Judgment | | Allocation Questionnaire

| | ▼

| | Allocation to Small Claims Track

| | ▼

| Rejected ▶ | Case considered under Small Claims Track

| | ▼

6. **Enforcement** (if Plaintiff wins) | Acce | JUDGMENT
  • Warrant of Execution   • Oral Examination
  • Garnishee Order   • Attachment of Earnings
  • Charging Order   • Bankruptcy Proceedings

- Property damage
- Disputes over services rendered
- Contract disputes

You cannot use the Small Claims Track in the County Court for possession proceedings. Any claim can be taken out of the Small Claims Track if the court decides the issues involved are too complex.

Winning without going to court

How do you win in court? One short answer is to avoid it. You can be a winner by resolving your dispute before you enter court. Litigation should be the last resort. The judicial system should be used only when all other alternatives fail. Why?

- Courts take time.
- Courts involve costs.
- Courts involve risk.

Before you issue proceedings, ask yourself if you have done everything reasonably possible to settle with the other party.

This Law Pack Guide will show you how best to win in court if you decide that the Small Claims Track is your only remedy. But winning in court is not easy. You may lose. You may not recover the full amount you are seeking. You may also have difficulty collecting your judgment.

Therefore, make every effort to settle your claim before going to court. There are four steps to settling out of court:

Step 1. Compromise

Contact the person you are having trouble with. Try to work matters out. A willingness to compromise is not a sign of weakness, but a sign of intelligence. A small compromise may allow you to settle the matter right away. People often refuse to settle matters because they have never been asked to. Ask!

An offer of compromise, made either orally or in writing, does not bind you if the compromise is not accepted. For example, if you tell your adversary that you will accept £500 of the £750 you feel is due, you can still issue proceedings for the original £750 if the offer is rejected. In order to negotiate without admitting liability, all letters and documents should be headed 'Without prejudice'.

Some important points about 'without prejudice' offers:

- You may offer to accept less without the other party using such an offer against you in court as long as you mark the offer 'without prejudice'. The concept is designed to encourage parties to reach a settlement.
- No correspondence can be shown to the District Judge if it is an offer to settle and is 'without prejudice'.
- If the other party accepts your 'without prejudice' offer, then that is a contract and both parties are bound by it.

Once you reach a compromise, put your agreement in writing. This avoids confusion about the terms of an oral agreement, and you will have proof of the settlement if there are any problems in collecting.

If you cannot reach a compromise, also put this in writing. This will show your good faith in attempting to settle rather than going to court. Some judges appreciate this effort.

Step 2. Demand letter

If you fail to compromise, your next step is to send your adversary a demand letter.

There are three reasons why a demand letter is essential:

1. It is useful in trying to settle your dispute.
2. You can use it as evidence in court.
3. It is a good way to outline your case before the judge.

The sole purpose of a demand letter is to resolve the problem. Write your letter tactfully. Do not alienate the other party. Be firm but polite. For instance, if you own a business, your letter should gently remind a forgetful debtor of his overdue bill. There is no need to be hostile.

Your demand letter should be brief and set forth the relevant facts of the dispute. Present your case logically. Write the letter so that it briefly reviews the entire dispute. Include in your letter your reply to any points the other party is likely to make.

You are not just writing to your adversary, because the judge may eventually see your letter. State your position so the judge can easily understand it. Remember, the judge does not know how your problem started or developed. Your letter may be the only way the judge becomes familiar with your position.

This is also important because the District Judge is likely to see your letter at the outset of the case and thus will be familiar with your

Highlight

In order to negotiate without admitting liability, all letters and documents should be headed 'Without prejudice'.

Example demand letter

133 Newington Park, London SE1 7PH
Tel: 0171 123 4567

11th May 1999

Nigel Smythe
22 Excalibur Way
London SE5 7QT

Dear Mr Smythe,

On the 10th October, 1998, I lent you £400 which you acknowledged by signing a promissory note (see enclosed copy). You promised to repay the £400 plus interest within sixty days. Ninety days have elapsed without payment from you. Your accrued debt is now £418 plus any expenses I may incur while pursuing this debt.

I am asking that you honour your promise immediately by remitting £418 to me. Please do this at once. If I have not received your payment in full within 24 hours from the date on this letter, I shall begin legal action.

Please remit your payment to the above address.

Yours sincerely,

argument before he or she is familiar with your adversary's case. If the other party never sets out his case in writing, this increases your chance of success.

Your demand letter must state that if you do not get satisfaction, you will go to court. Set a time limit for resolution but do not threaten. When setting time limits, always make them clearly identifiable, i.e., seven days from the date of this letter. Make the issuing of a summons your last resort.

Send two copies of your demand letter, one by first-class post and one by registered post so you can prove your letter was received. It is also a good idea to enclose a complete but unissued copy of your small claims summons form to show you are serious.

Keep several copies of your demand letter, and bring them to court with you. Give the judge a copy of your letter as part of your case.

Sometimes a debtor will be happy to reach a compromise settlement for less than the full amount. You too may feel that it is wiser to cut your losses and settle, but consider these three factors before you settle:

1. The strength of the case
2. The amount of time you are willing to spend on the case
3. The amount of money you are willing to spend on the case

If you settle your case after you have issued proceedings but before the hearing, make sure your settlement is in writing. Advise the court that you will not appear at your hearing.

If your settlement involves instalment payment, go to court and present your agreement to the judge. You may have a judgment or other order entered that complies with your settlement agreement. This way, if your agreement is not complied with, you can use the collection methods discussed later in this Guide. If a case has already been issued, never dismiss it until you have been paid in full.

Step 3. Telephone calls ━━━━━━

A telephone call is an alternative way of settling your claim. Calls can produce positive results because they are difficult to ignore. Often people are inclined to work out some type of payment arrangement there and then. Some people find it very difficult to face up to a problem. It is easy to ignore correspondence; it is not so easy to ignore telephone calls. People are very often relieved to settle an outstanding problem.

Speaking to your adversary may also help to resolve the matter amicably by giving him or her a chance to explain his or her reasons for not paying. But to succeed, your telephone calls must be reasonable and businesslike, not harassing or abusive.

Telephone calls require planning and preparation. Here are some steps to follow:

Be organised. Make sure you have everything necessary to discuss your claim in front of you. Review it one more time before you make the call.

Identify yourself. State your name and the reason for your call. If you are calling for a business, state your name, your title, and the name of the business.

Speak only to the debtor or the person in charge of handling your claim.

Give introductory information, including:

1. The claim you are referring to.
2. The exact amount owed.
3. When the debt was incurred.
4. How much time the debtor has had to pay.

Step 4. Successful settlement methods

To get paid without making a small claim requires some basic understanding of collection methods that work. Here are a few pointers:

► *Start by demanding payment in full.* Do not indicate that you may accept instalment or partial payments; insist upon immediate full payment of the debt. The debtor will undoubtedly give reasons why you are not entitled to full payment, or offer excuses for non-payment.

► *Encourage the debtor to make the first offer of settlement.* It may be for more than you would have been willing to accept.

► *Negotiate for instalments.* Often debtors simply do not have the money to pay all at once, though they could perhaps pay in instalments. But do reach precise agreement on how much will be paid and when. You should try to get as much as possible on the first payment.

If agreeing to instalments, always get the first payment immediately. Debtors will often agree to a payment schedule, then not pay when the time comes. This results in an unnecessary delay.

If you agree on a payment schedule, always make this condition: if any payment is not made on the due date, the full amount becomes due immediately.

► *Try for security.* Will the debtor offer security? Protect yourself in case the debtor later defaults on the promise to pay.

► *Request that the problem be resolved.* If you want specific action rather than money, ask for it. For example, if you want the company to fix your roof properly, say so. Make sure you direct your request to the person with the authority to make the decision you want.

► *Make the settlement sound appealing.* When a dispute is settled, there are savings on both sides. The creditor saves the time and expense of litigation. The debtor saves his credit rating and court costs. Make these advantages clear to your adversary.

► *Send a confirming letter.* Refer to your discussions and any verbal agreement. Outline all the points. Stress the date you expect payment.

► *Does the debtor belong* to an association or professional body? If so, contact it and ask if it can help bring pressure on the debtor. For instance, the Association of International Tour Operators operates a system of low-cost arbitration over complaints against one of its members. Check the terms of any written agreement (arbitration is discussed later in this guide).

► *Ignore lame excuses.* Is the debtor's cheque in the post? If this is the first time you have heard this story, give your debtor the benefit of the doubt and say you will wait one week to receive it.

Did the debtor lose his job? Suggest a modest repayment schedule until the debtor is employed again. But do verify the debtor's story.

A divorce? This has no effect upon your claim. Whoever was obliged to pay you before the divorce is still obliged to pay you after the divorce.

When you feel you can no longer work things out with your adversary you must leave him or her with four thoughts:

1. It is important to pay the debt.
2. The bill is overdue.
3. You will carry on with the process until the bill is paid.
4. He or she can work with you now or pay a judgment with interest and court costs later.

Claim disputes

In most instances the debtor knows money is owed to you, but cannot pay due to financial hardship and because other debts are more pressing. Patience and a repayment schedule can usually resolve these cases.

Highlight

Did the debtor lose his job? Suggest a modest repayment schedule until the debtor is employed again. But do verify the debtor's story.

Still, there are times when people have bona fide disputes. Was the roof properly fixed? Did the neighbour cause the damage to the fence? Is your custom-made dress a proper fit?

Do you have a winning case?

Before you go to court you must resolve two issues:

1. Can you win your case?
2. Can you collect on your judgment?

What makes a winning case? Liability. You will not get any money from a defendant until you prove that the defendant is legally responsible for your loss. This means that you must prove liability. Your loss is not enough to make a winning case; it must also be the other side's legal fault. You must state facts to the judge to show that the defendant should be held legally accountable.

The judge will listen to your evidence and decide whether you have a case. It is for you to establish the facts in as favourable a way as possible. The judge rules on the legal position.

However, if you understand some of the principles of the relevant law, it will aid your preparation and help ensure that your arguments are more easily understood and appreciated by the judge. This should increase your chances of success.

The following are some relevant causes of action:

Contract dispute. A valid contract signed by both parties has been broken by the other side and you have suffered monetary loss, e.g. an invoice has not been paid.

Negligence. The negligence of the defendant has resulted in property damage or loss that can be quantified, e.g. someone cuts down a tree which then falls on your car.

Landlord's failure to repair. Your landlord has not fixed a defective boiler or a leak.

Personal injury. The intentional or negligent behaviour of the defendant, e.g. a road accident, has caused you to suffer personal injury.

Defective product. You suffered loss due to a defective product and have the right of compensation from the supplier and/or the manufacturer.

Warranties. A written or implied warranty or guarantee has been breached and you have suffered a monetary loss.

Consumer claim. If you are an individual and bought defective or wrong goods or services from a business, your case may be covered by consumer legislation such as the Sale of Goods and Services Acts. These have specific rules relating to such claims that make it easier to prove them.

It is most important to show how the defendant's wrongful act caused you an actual injury that can be translated into a monetary recovery. Wrongdoing without harm is not usually entitled to compensation.

Can you collect?

Even if you win, your victory is worthless unless you can enforce the judgment. If your defendant is genuinely unable to pay, he or she may not be worth chasing, even if no defence is offered.

Unfortunately, there is no simple way to investigate the finances of a defendant unless you are prepared to pay for credit search, but this is seldom cost-effective in a small claims case. At best you can make enquiries, such as a court-ordered oral examination, to learn what you can about the defendant. You may find your adversary has more creditors, some of whom hold judgments ahead of yours. See Chapter 10 for more information on enforcing a judgment.

It is important to be practical. It makes no more sense to waste valuable time, effort, and court costs chasing an uncollectable debt than it does suing on a negligible claim.

The Small Claims Track only makes sense when you have a reasonable chance of winning and collecting enough money to make the exercise worthwhile.

Highlight

If your defendant is genuinely unable to pay, he or she may not be worth chasing, even if no defence is offered.

Courts and costs

Small claims cases are always dealt with in a County Court. You can start your claim in any County Court. However, the proceedings will be transferred automatically to the defendant's local court if:

  a) the defendant is an individual; and

  b) it is a liquidated claim, i.e., for a fixed sum such as a debt, and

  b) the defendant replies to the court intending to defend the claim.

You will be notified by the new court once the proceedings have been transferred.

If your claim is for unspecified damages, as in a personal injury case, the claim will not be transferred.

It is best to keep proceedings in your own County Court, particularly if the defendant lives some distance away.

How do you find a County Court? They are located throughout the country. Find one near you by referring to the telephone directory under 'Courts'. The courts are open Monday to Friday from 10 a.m. to 4 p.m.

There is a fee required to start a small claims case, so it is important to have confidence of recovery before you issue proceedings.

The exact amount you will be required to pay will depend upon the amount of your claim. Since the fees do change, it is best to have the court staff advise you what your fee will be when you issue proceedings. The defendant will be ordered to pay this fee if you win, but remember: you still have to recover the money from the defendant.

Costs

You can recover the following costs if you win your case:

- The fees paid to issue the case, for lodging the '*Allocation Questionnaire*' (discussed in Chapter 8) and for any applications.

- The fixed costs for issuing proceedings if you enlisted a solicitor's help. Currently these costs are between £25 and £62 depending upon how much you recover.

- The fees and some costs of enforcing your judgment.

- Any witness expenses, such as for travel and loss of earnings limited to £50 per day.

Apart from filing fees and possible solicitor fees, you may also incur witness expenses. This is necessary if a witness is needed to corroborate your story, testify as to events, or give an expert opinion. You must at least pay a witness's reasonable travel expenses to and from the court and also any lost wages. Expert witnesses will often expect a professional fee for their opinion; this may easily exceed any possible recovery from the case. If you use an expert you can only recover £200 for his fees if you win.

The case can be transferred by the judge out of the Small Claims Track to the Fast or Multi Tracks in circumstances where the judge feels it is too complex, legally and factually, even though its value is less than the current small claims limit. The winning party can, from the date of transfer, recover the legal costs of instructing a solicitor.

Conditional fees — personal injury cases
Solicitors are now allowed to act for clients on a conditional or 'no win, no fee' basis in personal injury cases. This means that if you win the case you pay them their normal costs plus a 'success fee'; if you lose the case you pay nothing. The success fee varies; at most it can be double the amount of normal costs, but cannot be based upon the solicitor taking a percentage of the damages. Remember that if you lose you may still have to pay the other side's fees if you are not within the small claims limit.

Some County Court fees as of 26th April 1999

Commencement of Proceedings

Monetary Claim	Fee
< £200	£20
£201–£300	£30
£301-£400	£40
£401-£500	£50
£501-£1000	£70
£1001-£5000	£100
Non-monetary Claim	£120

General Fees

Allocation Questionnaire filing	£80

Enforcement Fees

Garnishee	£50
Charging Order	£50
Warrant of Execution	
up to £125	£25
over £125	£45
Warrant for Possession	£80

Full details of County Court fees are available at the Court Service web site: **www.courtservice.gov.uk**

Who can sue?

If you are bringing a claim, you are the 'claimant'. The party you are suing is the 'defendant'. There can be multiple claimants and multiple defendants.

Any individual over the age of 18 can make a claim. Although a 'child' (i.e.under the age of 18) can only claim on his own behalf for unpaid wages, he can file a claim through a guardian or a parent.

An individual bringing a claim must state his full name, without initials. You may, as a business owner or operator, also bring a claim.

- If you are a firm, bring a claim using the firm's name, followed by the words 'a firm'. List the address of the firm.

    Example: Law Pack Publishing, a firm, 10 Cole Street, London, SE1 3AB.

- If you are a limited company, bring a claim using the name designation 'limited company' and either your trading address or the address of your registered office.

    Example: Law Pack Publishing Limited, a limited company, 10 Cole Street, London, SE1 3AB.

- If you are a person doing business under another name, bring a claim using your own name followed by the words 'trading as', and the address of the business.

    Example: John Doe, trading as Law Pack Publishing, 10 Cole Street, London, SE1 3AB.

Who can be sued?

You can sue just about anyone.

Always take care to consider who you name on the summons. If you name the wrong party, the claim may be struck out and costs ordered against you. If in doubt seek advice from the court, or Citizens' Advice Bureau.

The following are general rules regarding whom you may sue.

Highlight

If you name the wrong party, the claim may be struck out and costs ordered against you.

Suing one person

If you are suing an individual, use the most complete name you have for that person. Include title (Mr., Mrs., Dr., etc) and all known forenames and surname; full residential address and telephone number in England and Wales.

Suing two or more people

If you are suing more than one person on a claim arising from a single incident, list and serve each person. For example, if you are suing John Doe and John Smith for the £1,000 they borrowed from you, list them as follows: 'John Doe and John Smith'. This is also required for a husband and wife; do not list them as 'Mr. and Mrs. Smith', but as 'John Smith and Joan Smith'. Additionally, each defendant must be served separately. Service of process will be discussed in a later section.

If you are suing more than one person on two claims, you must sue each one in a separate action under the Small Claims Track.

Suing a sole trader

If you are suing a sole trader, list the name of the owner and the name of the business. This would be as follows: 'John Doe, trading as ABC Painting'. Make sure you know who the true owner of the business is before you sue. A judgment against an incorrect defendant is worth very little.

Suing a firm

If you are suing a partnership, you have a choice of suing either the individual partners or the partnership itself.

The advantages of suing the partnership rather than the individuals are:

- service is easier and the proceedings are simpler.
- judgment can be enforced against partnership property without special permission of the judge, or 'leave'.
- judgment can be enforced without leave against the personal property of any person who is identified as a partner in the proceedings.

All partners are individually liable for all the debts of the business, so you need not specify the partner with whom you dealt.

List the partnership as follows: 'ABC Painting, a firm', followed by the address.

CHAPTER 5

Highlight

Try to get a judgment against more than one person. In the event you have trouble collecting from one partner, you may be able to collect from other partners.

Try to get a judgment against more than one person. In the event you have trouble collecting from one partner, you may be able to collect from other partners.

Suing a limited company

If you are suing a limited company, list its full name and address. Example: 'ABC Painting, Ltd., a limited company, 32 Cole Street, London, SE1 3AB'.

A limited company is considered a person. This means that you can sue and enforce a judgment against a company. Do not sue the owners of the limited company or its managing director individually unless you have a personal claim against them that is separate from their role as part of the limited company. Usually, people who own or operate a limited company are not liable for its corporate debts. This is known as 'limited liability' and is the advantage to forming a limited company.

Suing a child

While anyone under 18 cannot sue by themselves (except for wages), they can be sued. If your defendant is a child, i.e. under 18, you should specify this as follows: 'James Smith, a child by [*insert name of parent currently responsible for him/her*] ... his/her litigation friend'. It would be wise to check whether the parents have legal responsibility for the acts or debts of the child. If they do, they should also be named as defendants.

6

How much should you sue for?

If your claim exceeds the amount currently allowed using the Small Claims Track, you must either reduce your claim or bring your action in another track. If you can show that your claim is in fact two separate claims, you may to recover more than the current limit. But you are not allowed to divide a claim that is over the limit into two or more claims so that each is within the limit.

For example, 'A' lent 'B' £5,500. B was to repay A in two instalments, each for £2,250. A cannot argue that there were two separate contracts. The loan was one transaction so A may not have two claims heard in the court using the Small Claims Track.

The legal way to divide your claim is to bring multiple actions against the same person based on different claims. Refer to the causes of action discussed in Chapter 3. Here are some examples of causes of action:

- Contract dispute
- Negligence
- Personal injury
- Defective product
- Warranty
- Consumer claim

Try to present your loss as separate legal claims. For instance, you may be able to argue that £6,000 in damages actually involves two or more separate claims, such as two or more contracts, or one contract plus an injury to your person or property.

For example:

A is a painter and is owed £6,000 by B for work done. A sues B for failure to pay. A can claim there were three contracts, and thus three claims: one for failure to pay for the paint (£400); one for failure to pay for painting B's house (£3,000); and one for failure to pay for the hiring of scaffolding (£2,600). By arguing three separate contracts, A may be able to collect more than the £5,000 limit in Small Claims Court by dividing the damages (which total £6,000) among three separate claims.

Calculating the size of your claim

When in doubt, overestimate your damages slightly. If you are unsure as to the exact amount of your claim, always issue your action for higher damages than you believe you are entitled to. The judge has the power to award you less than you request, but will never award you more.

If you find yourself in court and realise you have asked for too little, request that the judge allow you to amend your claim and, if necessary, continue your case at a later date.

It is easy to calculate the amount you are entitled to. The following are some examples of how the exact amount of a claim may be calculated:

Contract disputes

To arrive at the exact figure for a contract claim, work out the difference between the amount you were supposed to receive under the contract and what you actually received. For example, if A was to paint B's house for £1,000 and B paid only A £750, A has a claim against B for £250.

Interest

You can claim interest on all money due to you, whether your claim is for a fixed amount or damages are to be assessed.

- If you have a contract that specifies how interest is charged, base your interest claim on that. But remember, you must state that the rate of interest you are claiming is agreed; refer to the contract and the clause dealing with interest.

- Otherwise, all debts carry a fixed interest at the judgment rate, which is currently 8 per cent per annum. Prior to 1st April 1993 it was 15 per cent per annum; if the debt was due prior to this date you can claim the higher rate until 1st April 1993 and the lower rate thereafter.

- Damages, once assessed, are awarded interest at a rate the judge decides is reasonable.

Interest is calculated from the date the debt became due. If it became due over a period of time (instalments), you can either stagger the interest or calculate on the whole sum from the date the last amount became due.

Interest continues to be due until payment is made or until the date of your judgment. Interest does not carry on after judgment unless the amount of the judgment is over £5,000.

Note: You have to include the interest due in the amount being claimed, which means it forms part of the £5,000 small claims limit. If you were claiming £4,850 with interest of £275, your total claim would be outside the automatic limit of the Small Claims Track. But you could limit your claim to £5,000 in order to use the Small Claims Track.

Be sure that your damages include only the amount of money you are owed. Do not try to collect money in court that you have already recovered from someone else. See personal injury cases, below.

Property damage
The exact amount of your claim for property damage is usually the amount of money it would take to fix the damaged item. For example, if A's car was dented by B, A would sue B for the amount it would cost to repair it. To be safe, A should get several estimates.

If the cost to repair the damaged item exceeds the value of the item, you may be entitled only to the value of the item. If the cost to fix A's dented car exceeds the market value of A's car before the accident, A may be entitled to sue B only for the market value of the car. This depends upon factors such as whether the item is easily replaceable.

If you are entitled only to the fair market value of the item, you must deduct the value of the object after the injury. If the fair market value of A's car is £1,000 and it would cost £1,200 to repair the dent, A may sue for £1,000 (the value of the car). However, the value of the car after the dent must be deducted from that amount. If A's car is now worth £100 with the dent, that amount must be deducted from the £1,000 fair market value of A's car. This means A's damages are £900.

Think of it this way: if the cost of repair exceeds the value of the object, you are likely to be limited to the fair market value of the object less the value of the object after damage.

However, if the value of the damaged object exceeds the cost of repair, you are entitled to sue for the cost of the repair. If A's car is worth £5,000 and the dent cost £500 to repair, A's claim is for £500.

Be prepared to show the actual value of your property in court. How do you do this? The best way is to get estimates from experts in the field and have these experts testify in court. Alternatively, they can put the value of your property in writing. You may also want to confirm your expert's estimate with newspaper ads for comparable goods.

Highlight

Be prepared to show the actual value of your property in court. You may also want to confirm your expert's estimates with newspaper ads for comparable goods.

To calculate the amount of your claim, determine:

1. The value of the item before the accident.
2. How much it will cost to repair.
3. What the item is worth now that it is damaged.

If 2 is less than 1, claim for 2. If 2 is more than 1, claim for 1 minus 3.

Damage to clothing

The Small Claims Track is frequently used in cases involving clothing. However, claims involving clothing damage differ from other property damage cases because your own items of clothing have little value to anyone else, even if in good condition.

If your damaged clothing was new or almost new, sue for its cost. For example, if your dry-cleaner damaged your new £200 suit, sue for £200.

If your clothing was not new, sue for the percentage of remaining value of the clothing. This reflects how worn it was when the damage occurred. For example, your dry-cleaner damaged your suit that cost £200 two years ago. You have been wearing the suit fairly regularly and feel it would have lasted another two years. Since the suit had lost half of its useable life, you should sue for £100.

Personal injury cases

Few personal injury cases go to Small Claims Court, because the amount of the claims are usually much higher than the £5,000 small claims limit for personal injury. However, any personal injury case claiming £5,000 or less can be heard in Small Claims Court.

To work out the exact amount of your personal injury claim, also consider:

1. Out-of-pocket expenses
2. Loss of pay or vacation time
3. Damage to property
4. Pain and suffering (to be assessed by the judge)

Remember, you cannot collect money in court that you have already recovered from someone else. If your employer paid you for the days you missed work, do not expect to recover for lost wages. If you have received any state benefits, these also must be disclosed and taken into account.

The small claims limits for personal injury cases are different because it is recognised that they often take more work and involve greater costs to prove the claim, especially medical reports, which are largely unrecoverable in small claims.

For this reason a personal injury matter can only be dealt with as a small claim where the total claim is less than £5,000 and of that no more than £1,000 is sought for general damages to your person, for example, if you claimed £2,000 for loss of earnings, £250 for damage to your clothing and £1,000 for a broken leg.

Be prepared to provide the judge with proof of your out-of-pocket expenses, such as medical bills, fares for visiting hospital, receipts, etc.

If you decide to claim over the personal injury limits, special rules apply to personal injury matters. Consult a Citizens' Advice Bureau or a solicitor.

Pain and suffering

Pain and suffering is the discomfort and inconvenience caused by your injury. The court calculates the amount of these damages by considering other cases of a similar nature. You can approximate the amount by checking recent case law. The easiest way to do this is to look in the reference section of your local library for a book called *Kemp & Kemp: Quantum of Damages*. This lists different types of injury and the awards made. Find a similar case and increase your award amount by at least the rate of inflation. Show a copy to the court when they are assessing the damages.

Highlight

Be prepared to provide the judge with proof of your out-of-pocket expenses, such as medical bills, fares for visiting hospital, receipts, etc.

Starting the procedure

It is not difficult to start a claim using the Small Claims Track. This guide contains completed examples of all the necessary forms, as well as instructions. Contact your local County Court to obtain blank copies of the forms. You can also fill in and print copies from the government Court Service web site: **www.courtservice.gov.uk**. The court staff, Consumer Advice Centres and the Citizens' Advice Bureau also can be very helpful.

You will need three copies of the *Claim Form N1*. One copy is for the defendant, one for the court and one for yourself. If there is more than one defendant you will need an additional copy of the form for each additional defendant. Read the *Notes for Claimant Form N1A* on completing the *Claim Form* (see page 66 for example).

Once you have fully completed *Form N1* you will need to give it to the court staff together with a fee. You can issue proceedings by going to court in person or by sending your *Form N1* by post.

You will receive, in return, a receipt for your fee called a *Notice of Issue Form N205A*. This also gives you your case number, so you must keep this document carefully.

You have now started the proceedings. The next step is to serve the summons on the defendant.

Serving the defendant

The defendant must be served with a copy of the *Claim Form N1* that you have issued, along with the *Reponse Pack Form N9* which the court sends. The *Response Pack* includes forms *N9A*, *N9B*, *N9C* and *N9D* (forms *N9C* and *N9D* are used where the claim is for an unspecified amount or is not a claim for money). Forms *N9A* and *N9B* allow the defendant to admit to the amount claimed in full or part and, if necessary, propose a plan for paying the money due. He may also state his defence (see pages 72-74 for examples).

Who can serve?

The defendant may be served the claim form in two ways:

1. The court can be asked to serve the defendant, which they will do by first-class post.

2. You may arrange to serve the defendant personally yourself, by using a firm of process servers or via any other person or by sending it by first-class post.

How to serve the defendant yourself

There are four principal options available to you if you wish to serve the defendant yourself:

1. Personally serve the defendant by handing the claim form and the reply forms to him.

2. By first-class post to the defendant.

3. By leaving it at the last known address of the defendant.

4. Send the reply forms and claim form to the defendant's solicitor if the defendant has already instructed one. The solicitor must agree to accept service of the claim form.

It is also possible to serve by fax provided that you have the defendant's agreement to do so and the fax number to which it is to be sent. Both the agreement and the fax number must be in writing from the defendant.

Service by e-mail is only available where both sides have legal representatives acting for them.

It is best to leave service to the court, unless there is some degree of urgency. Although the court usually takes a couple of weeks to serve the claim form, you are assured that the process is done correctly. The court rules relating to service can be complex and their interpretation strict. It is also easier to enter judgment if no response is received if the court served the summons.

Defendant's response

Once the claim form is served, strict time limits must be adhered to.

The defendant has 14 days after he or she is actually or is deemed served to return one of the options from the *Response Pack N9*. If the defendant fails to return the forms within the time limit, you can enter judgment in default.

If service is on the defendant's solicitor, they having agreed to accept service, the defendant is deemed served 2 working days after the claim form is posted.

CHAPTER 7

If you are serving yourself, then service is deemed as follows:

► If handed to the defendant — the time at which handed to them.
► If sent by post — the second day after posting.
► If left at an address — the day after delivery to the address.
► If by fax — if on a business day before 4.00 p.m. that day; otherwise the next business day.

If the court is serving the defendant, it will note on *Notice of Issue Form N205A* the date of service, deemed to be two days after posting.

It is possible the defendant will not receive your claim form. If the defendant moved or you gave the incorrect address, the Post Office will return the claim form to the sender. If it was serving for you, the court will then advise you of this by sending you a *Notice of Non-Service N216* and ask you to effect service.

If you are serving the defendant personally, you must deliver the claim form to the defendant within four months from when you issued your claim, or you must seek permission from the court to extend the time for service. This extension is ordinarily granted when the court believes you are making a diligent effort to find the defendant.

Alternatively, you may withdraw your claim, allowing you time to locate the defendant and issue your claim again. This involves paying the issue fee again.

After service

The defendant has five options once the claim form is received:

1. Attempt to settle the claim.
2. Admit owing all the money claimed.
3. Admit owing some of the money claimed.
4. Deny owing the money claimed.
5. Ignore the claim form.

Let us examine each situation:

The defendant wants to settle

This happens in many cases. Unfortunately, it may take a claim form to convince a defendant you are serious about collecting. Many people will call your bluff until the claim form arrives, at which point they can no longer afford to ignore you.

Should the defendant approach you to settle, follow the suggestions in Chapter 2 of this guide. You may wish to add on additional costs at this point. After all, you have already started your proceedings; your settlement should reflect the inconvenience and costs involved.

After a defence has been returned to the court, when returning the *Allocation Questionnaire* (see page 42), the parties may request a one month stay in the proceedings to allow for a settlement to be agreed. The court can order such a stay if both parties ask for it or if the court considers it is appropriate. The purpose of this is simply to focus the parties' minds on settlement now, before a hearing is listed.

The defendant admits owing money

The defendant does not often admit to owing the full claim. It happens when the defendant knows he has no valid defence to the claim, and usually just needs time to pay it.

If he or she is admitting to the full claim, the defendant will complete *Form N9A (admission)*, which he or she received with the claim form. The defendant sends the admission directly to you rather than to the court.

On question 11 on the form, the defendant will probably propose a repayment schedule to repay the debt. You now have three choices:

1. Accept the defendant's payment proposal.
Ask the court to send the defendant an order to pay you the proposed instalments. This is called 'entering judgment on acceptance'. Complete the *Request for Judgment* on the lower portion of *Form N205A*, which is then sent to the court. The court uses the information on *Form N205A* to complete the judgment order.

2. State how you want the defendant to pay.
If the defendant admits owing you money but has not proposed how to pay the debt, you can ask for the judgment to be paid in instalments or in one payment by ticking the appropriate box in section C of *Form N205A*.

3. Refuse the defendant's offer to pay.
To object to the defendant's payment proposal you must state on the lower portion of the back of *Form N205A* why you object and what you would be willing to accept. Return this to the court, which will review the defendant's proposal and your reply and decide how the defendant will pay. This is called 'entering a judgment by determination'.

You are not bound by the court's decision concerning the defendant's repayment proposal. You can request to have a District Judge review the court's decision by asking for an appointment. To do this, complete an *Application Notice Form N244* (see page 83), or send a letter stating why you object to the repayment schedule approved by the court officer. You must pay a fee, currently £50, for such an application.

The court then returns to you a copy of your *Form N244* with details of the place and date of your appointment with the District Judge. You and the defendant will confer informally in the District Judge's chambers.

Essentially, the District Judge will ask you both questions and then make a decision as to whether the defendant can afford faster repayments or why you cannot show greater patience in receiving your money. The judge, of course, will try to resolve the claim by satisfying both of you.

The judge may immediately advise you of his decision or reserve judgment. In any event, if the judge decides to change the repayment schedule, both you and the defendant will receive notification reflecting the new repayment schedule the defendant is to follow.

Unless you have information proving that the defendant has not fully disclosed his or her income, it is generally not wise to seek a review by

Highlight

You are not bound by the court's decision concerning the defendant's repayment proposal. You can request to have a District Judge review the court's decision by asking for an appointment.

a District Judge. Judges are extremely reluctant to override decisions made by the court staff. Consider abiding by the decision of the court staff regarding a fair repayment schedule.

The defendant admits owing some money

If the defendant admits to only part of your claim, he will fill in *Form N9B (defence)* and *Form N9A (admission)*. If he has already paid the amount admitted, he need not fill in *Form N9B*.

The reply forms are then sent to the court by the defendant. The court will send you copies along with *Form N225A Notice of Part Admission*.

Form N9A gives you financial information about the defendant's ability to pay that portion of the debt admitted as owing. *Form N9B* states the defence to that portion of the claim the defendant denies owing.

At this point you may either:

1. Accept the defendant's admission of partial liability.
2. Contest the defendant's admission of partial liability and continue to sue for your full claim.

Highlight

Sometimes the defendant proposes to pay the amount offered immediately. If the defendant is silent on the method of payment, you can request immediate payment.

If you decide to accept the defendant's offer of partial payment, you will want the court to enter 'judgment on acceptance'. Complete *Form N225A*, and return it to the court within 14 days.

Sometimes the defendant proposes to pay the amount offered immediately. If the defendant is silent on the method of payment, you can request immediate payment.

More often the defendant will propose a repayment schedule. You are now asked to accept a part of your claim as full payment and be paid that amount over an extended time.

If you agree with the defendant's repayment schedule, indicate this on *Form N225A*. The court will issue *Judgment for Claimant* and send copies to you and the defendant to confirm how much will be paid, and when it will be paid.

If you agree with the amount but disagree with how the defendant proposes to pay it, you should explain on *Form N205A* why you object to the defendant's offer, what you will accept and how quickly you want to be paid.

The process from this point is exactly the same as if the defendant agreed to your entire claim but wants more time to pay it than you are willing to accept.

The defendant denies owing money ━━━

If the defendant disagrees with all of your claim, he or she must state the reason on *Form N9B (defence)*. If the defendant denies only part of your claim (partial admission), he or she must complete and return to the court both *Form N9A (admission)* and *Form N9B (defence)*. You will be sent both forms by the court together with *Form N225*.

If the defendant asserts that your claim has already been fully paid (expressed as 'the amount claimed has been paid'), the court will send you copies of defendant's *Form N9B*.

Once a defence is received, an *Allocation Questionnaire N150* is sent to you and the defendant, which must be completed and returned by both parties within 14 days. See page 77 for example. As the claimant, you must pay a fee when returning the questionnaire, currently £80.

Filling in the Allocation Questionnaire

Box A — Settlement
This stay is only automatic where BOTH sides ask for it. Unless you have reason to believe the defendant is asking for it and is genuine in so doing, it is best to put 'No'. The court may order a stay, whether or not all the other parties to the case agree. Where a stay is granted, it will be for an initial period which the judge will specify.

Box B — Track: this will be 'small claims'.

Box C — Pre-action protocols
For certain kinds of claim, there are protocols which set out what ought to be done before court proceedings are issued. As at April 1999 there are protocols for clinical negligence and personal injury claims only. Other protocols may be introduced later.

Box D — Applications
If you intend to apply for summary judgment or make any other application, you should, if you have not already done so, file the application with your completed *Allocation Questionnaire*.

Box E — Witnesses of fact
Include anyone whose evidence you will need to prove your case. If the defendant in his defence admits some aspects of your claim you do not need to prove them again. Remember to include yourself (if you will be giving evidence) but not experts (who should be included in Section F).

Box F — Experts
If it is your case that someone has done a bad job, then you may need an

Highlight

Once a defence is received, an *Allocation Questionnaire N150* is sent to all parties, which must be completed and returned within 14 days.

expert to confirm to the court that this is so. Remember you can only recover a limited amount of the costs of an expert in small claims.

Box G — Location of trial
You can request a County Court outside the area of the current case. If, for instance, there were a number of witnesses and they all live near another court.

Box H — Representation and estimate of trial time
Give your best estimate of how long it will take.

Box I — Costs
As this is a small claims matter, only show those costs which will be recoverable. See page 23 for information on recoverable costs.

Box J — Other information
Give any other information that you think is relevant here. If, for instance, there is something special about your case, then say so here. For example:

- ► If you want to show video evidence.
- ► If an interpreter is needed.
- ► If you want the court to make a site visit.

Remember, as claimant you should include the fee of £80 when returning the *Questionnaire*.

Once the court receives both *N150*s, it will be referred to a District Judge for allocation. The District Judge can:

1. Determine your case is too complex to be dealt with informally under the Small Claims Track and order an allocation to the Fast or Multi Track.
2. Set a preliminary hearing to consider making special directions; or
3. Set a small claims hearing.

Allocation to Fast or Multi Track
The District Judge's decision to order allocation to the Fast or Multi track can be made when he or she first reviews your file, or after an appointment (conference) or arbitration hearing proves unsuccessful. In the latter instances you do not have to agree to go to trial, but the mere threat of an open court trial may be sufficient for you and the defendant to resolve your differences.

Transfer to another track will result in a full trial before a Circuit Judge in open court. Such trials are considerably more formal than regular small claims tracks and may require a solicitor. The cost of a solicitor may outweigh any benefits of proceeding in open court. Furthermore, if you lose in open court you may be ordered to pay for the defendant's solicitor; the defendant may similarly be liable to pay the costs of your solicitor if you win.

Considering the £5,000 limit on small claims cases, you should reconsider your case very carefully if re-allocation is proposed.

A preliminary hearing
The court may hold a preliminary hearing for the consideration of the claim, but only where:

- It considers that special directions are needed to ensure a fair hearing; and it appears necessary for a party to attend at court to ensure that he understands what he must do to comply with the special directions.
- The court is to dispose of the claim as one side has no real prospect of success at a final hearing.

Directions
The court will at this stage give the standard directions which are:

1. Each party shall deliver to every other party and to the court office copies of all documents (including any expert's report) on which he intends to rely at the hearing no later than [   ] [14 days before the hearing].
2. The original documents shall be brought to the hearing.
3. [Notice of hearing date and time allowed].
4. The court must be informed immediately if the case is settled by agreement before the hearing date.

Special directions
These may be necessary in certain types of case such as:

- road traffic accidents
- building disputes
- landlord and tenant disputes
- holiday claims

and they may deal with such matters as:

- expert evidence
- exchange of witness statements or documents
- provision of plans and photographs

Highlight

Considering the £5,000 limit on small claims cases, you should reconsider your case very carefully if re-allocation is proposed.

If you feel there are any reasons why your case should have a preliminary hearing, ask for this and give the reasons why when you return the *Allocation Questionnaire*.

The Small Claims hearing

On the matter being allocated to the Small Claims Track, the court sends a *Notice of Allocation Form*, stating the date and time of the hearing along with an explanation of how to prepare for it.

The hearing is held before an arbitrator (usually a District Judge), who listens to each party's case and decides who is right based on the evidence presented. Evidence may include verbal statements, written documents or expert testimony. You will be given guidance on how to prepare and present your case in the next chapter.

After the hearing, the court will inform you and the defendant of the arbitrator's decision (or 'award') that states who must pay, the amount to be paid and the manner of payment. The court will later write to you confirming the award made.

You and the defendant each have the right to appeal the arbitrator's decision, but your appeal will be successful only if you can show that the arbitrator applied the law incorrectly or did not conduct the hearing properly. The arbitrator's findings of facts cannot be appealed.

The defendant ignores the claim

The defendant must return *Acknowledgement of Service Form* to the court within 14 days of the effective date of service.

It is not uncommon for the defendant to fail to reply to the claim within the 14 days. The defendant may feel he is without a defence, has no assets to lose, or both.

Default judgment

If there is no reply within the time limit, you should ask the court to enter judgment by default. Complete and return to the court Sections A and C on the *Notice of Issue Form N205A* or *Request for Judgment and Reply to Admission Form N225*. Pay particular attention to how you want the judgment paid. You will naturally want payment at once, but may be more successful in collecting if you grant reasonable instalments. Always request payment in full.

The court will complete *Judgment for Claimant Form N30* advising the defendant of the judgment against him, the amount, how it is to be paid,

---

Highlight

If you feel there are any reasons why your case should have a preliminary hearing, ask for this and give the reasons why when you return the *Allocation Questionnaire*.

Highlight

It is not uncommon for the defendant to fail to reply to the claim within the 14 days. The defendant may feel he is without a defence, has no assets to lose, or both.

and where payment shall be directed. You will receive a sealed copy of your judgment against the defendant.

The defendant can, though, apply to the court to set aside a judgment entered in default. He must explain why he failed to respond to it and why he disputes it. The court may set aside a judgment if it is satisfied the defendant has a real prospect of successfully defending the claim or if it is satisfied there is some other good reason. If the court agrees to set it aside the defendant will be allowed to defend the matter and it will then go to a hearing. If this happens you can ask the court to make the setting aside conditional upon the defendant paying the amount in dispute to the court. If this is done you then have the safety of the money being immediately available if you succeed at the arbitration hearing without the need for taking any enforcement action.

However, as already mentioned, obtaining judgment is the easy part. See the section 'Enforcing your judgment' for the steps to enforce the court's decision.

Winning your case

Familiarity with the Small Claims Track will not ensure victory. You must know how to present a winning case. In this section you will find the methods to improve your chances of winning a small claims case, whether you are the claimant or the defendant.

Preparing your case

Whether your case will be heard through informal appointment, arbitration or open court trial, you must know how to present a winning case. That means preparation.

It is essential to assemble the critical facts concerning your dispute, including evidence, witnesses, exhibits, documents and any other elements needed to prove your case.

Depending on the nature of your complaint you will need:

- Written contracts, estimates, proposals or bids.
- Letters and correspondence between you and your adversary.
- Any bills, whether paid or unpaid, as well as cancelled cheques, receipts or other evidence of payment.
- In personal injury cases, medical reports and certification of injury from your doctor, as well as medical bills.
- If you could not work due to these injuries, certification of absence from your employer as well as a statement of lost wages.
- If relevant, photographs of any injuries to yourself or damage to your property.
- In landlord/tenant cases, copies of your lease, rent receipts, security deposits or cleaning fees; invoices for repairs you have had done; photographs of the state and condition of the property.
- Witnesses willing to testify for you, or to give you a sworn affidavit.
- If the dispute involves a road accident, a sketch (or photograph) of the accident site.
- A timetable of important events.

To save time at the hearing, send advance copies of your written documents, photographs and sketches to the defendant, asking him to agree to their authenticity and accuracy. Once he agrees, he may not prolong the proceedings by raising such objections in a hearing or courtroom.

Assemble your documents and prepare a sequence of facts that includes:

- A list of witnesses and the statements each will make
- A list of documents you will introduce at the hearing
- A list of statements you will make in presenting your case

Then reverse your role and anticipate your adversary's case by listing the witnesses, statements and arguments you believe your adversary will use. With this completed, list the questions you will ask your adversary in order to disprove his statements. Finally, assemble the documents that show that your adversary's statements are incorrect.

Remember, you may present three categories of evidence:

1. **Physical evidence** – such as damaged property, documents, contracts, receipts, photographs, etc.
2. **Spoken evidence** – the statements of testimony given by you or others who are familiar with certain facts of the case.
3. **Expert evidence** – the testimony of an expert with professional qualifications. Remember you need the leave of the court to call an expert. If you think you will need one, ask for this on the *Allocation Questionnaire*.

Presenting your case

Good preparation and a clear, logical presentation are essential to winning your case. If you have prepared your case thoroughly you greatly improve your chances of success.

Remember, using the Small Claims Track is for amateurs. The court does not expect you to act as a professional lawyer. As an amateur you can greatly improve your chances of winning by following these ten tips:

1. Practise your presentation
It is a good idea to practise your court presentation at home before family or friends. If they clearly understand your points, it is likely the judge will.

2. Visit a court hearing
If the court allows it, attend a small claims hearing. Keep in mind that a preliminary hearing and arbitration are far less formal and are held in the

judge's chambers. You will largely respond to the judge's questions rather than present a court case and cross-examination. When you become familiar with the judge's practices, you may change your planned presentation.

3. Act properly

Appear at court punctually and dress appropriately. Always talk directly to the judge, not to your adversary. Address the judge as 'Sir', 'Madam' or 'Judge'. Most importantly, refer to your adversary courteously. A judge cannot rule in your favour simply because you are well-mannered, but your good demeanour can only reflect well on you. Do not interrupt the judge or your adversary. The judge will always allow you to answer when he has finished.

4. Be prepared

Prepare what you are going to say as a written speech, but do not read it. Practise it with a friend and ask for helpful criticism. Be sure to note and answer any questions that may arise.

5. Do not be too legalistic

Present the facts; do not argue the law. You are not a lawyer and the court does not expect a legal discourse. The judge will apply the law to the facts of your case.

Be reasonable. Do not paint a one-sided picture. District Judges are experienced at seeing both sides and will be more impressed by a party who presents a fair case. If you have a weak point, do not ignore it, but explain it in the most favourable way you can.

6. Use witnesses properly

If any facts in the case are in dispute, you must prove your version is correct by referring to documents or by using another person's testimony. Witnesses must be called to the court to give evidence. They may appear in person or, if agreed to by the other side, give testimony in a signed statement that is presented to the court in lieu of an appearance.

A reluctant witness can be forced to appear in court by using a court-issued witness summons. The summons must be issued at least seven days before the trial. There is a charge to have the court serve the summons.

You are also responsible to pay your witness's travel and other expenses. If you have several witnesses, ask the most willing and persuasive to appear. Obtain written statements from the others. If you need expert witnesses on technical matters, the Citizens' Advice Bureau may refer

Highlight

Always talk directly to the judge, not to your adversary. Address the judge as 'Sir', 'Madam' or 'Judge'.

you to one. The court may also allow an independent expert to serve as arbitrator instead of the District Judge.

7. Detail your case

Make it as difficult as you can for the defendant by being fully prepared. You will be less likely to forget an item if you note in advance all the dates, amounts and other major points you want to make. As the claimant you have to prove your case. By doing so you force the defendant to work hard to defend himself.

8. Keep your documents in order

Assemble your documents in chronological order and cross-index them by their order of presentation. Make copies of your documents for the judge and your adversary. If you have statements from witnesses, make certain they are signed and dated. If there are more than just a few pages, number them to enable the judge and your adversary to follow your presentation. Organisation makes it easier for you to answer questions.

Once you are in court, relax and talk slowly. Do not rush. When your adversary is talking, make notes of those points you will need to refer to. Wait until he has finished before replying.

9. Recording the hearing

All small claims hearings can be tape recorded by the court, but you may not record them yourself. If you think you may need this facility, ask for it before or at the beginning of the hearing.

The judge may direct that all or any part of the proceedings will be tape recorded by the court. A party may obtain a transcript of such a recording on payment of the proper transcriber's charges.

The judge will make a note of the central points of the oral evidence unless it is tape recorded by the court. A party is entitled to a copy of any note made by the judge.

10. Who says what when?

As already explained, small claims hearings usually take place in the District Judge's room, or 'chambers'.

Although the hearing is informal, it is nonetheless a court hearing in front of a judge, and you should follow the guidelines set out below. The hearing is in public and it is possible that members of the public can attend, although it is unlikely.

The parties sit either side of the judge at a table.

Highlight

Make it as difficult as you can for the defendant by being fully prepared.

11.   *Who may appear?*

A party may present his own case at a hearing, or a lawyer or lay representative may present it for him. A lay representative may only do so if the party is present at the hearing or if he is that party's employee or if the court gives permission. Any of its officers or employees may represent a corporate party.

As the claimant, you present your case first. Explain to the judge briefly what your claim is about and what you want from the defendant. Take the judge through any documents you have and then call your witnesses.

Once you have finished with each witness, the defendant may cross-examine him or her. After this you may again question the witness if the cross-examination raised any new points or if you need to clarify any earlier points.

The defendant answers your case by presenting his version of events and setting out those areas of your case he disagrees with, again referring to any supporting documents and calling any witnesses.

Both parties present a final summation, and the judge makes his decision. The judge usually does this immediately, but may want to consider the matter and decide later. The court will keep a written record of the judge's decision, which explains why you won or lost. This is important if you consider an appeal.

If you are unsure about anything that has happened, question the judge before you leave chambers.

Enforcing your judgment

Obtaining a judgment may be easier than getting paid. In some cases a debtor will have few, if any, assets from which to satisfy a judgment. In others, the debtor will simply refuse to pay, leaving it to you to enforce judgment.

There are several ways to enforce your small claims judgment. It is important to remember that attempts to enforce a judgment are impractical unless you are confident the debtor can pay the debt. This guide does not advocate the Small Claims Track if the debt is ultimately uncollectable.

Check whether there are other outstanding judgments against the debtor. All unpaid judgments are automatically registered at Registry of County Court Judgments (tel: 0171 380 0133). For a nominal fee they will tell you whether the debtor has other unsatisfied judgments. If there are many outstanding judgments against the debtor, your chances of getting paid are slight.

Your enforcement tactics depend on your debtor's situation. Is it likely that he will be able to pay? Is he employed? Does he have a building society or bank account?

It is always best to encourage voluntary payment from the debtor. You may do this directly with the debtor or ask the court to issue an instalment order. If the debtor asks for an instalment order, you may inquire about the debtor's assets to determine his or her ability to pay.

What are the methods for enforcing payment on a judgment? There are four:

1. Warrant of execution
2. Attachment of earnings order
3. Garnishee proceeding
4. Charging order

Warrant of execution

A warrant of execution orders County Court bailiffs to seize the debtor's personal belongings. Such belongings are then sold and the proceeds paid to you up to the value of your judgment.

But this method is not effective unless you know that the debtor has assets of value and you can direct the bailiffs to the assets by providing addresses. Bailiffs are only able to act on information you supply. They do not carry out any investigations. Personal items, such as clothes and tools of the debtor's trade, cannot be seized.

If there are insufficient assets, the bailiff will notify the court and you will be so advised.

Frequently, the debtor facing a warrant will apply to the court to suspend the warrant and allow him further time to pay the judgment. If the registrar should suspend the warrant, you may ask to have it reinstated if the debtor does not pay.

A warrant of execution remains in force for one year, but you may renew it continuously upon application to the court.

To issue a warrant of execution, send the following to the court:

- a copy of your judgment
- a completed *Form N323*, (see page 82 for example)
- the appropriate fee

Attachment of earnings

A more direct way to collect is to have the court order the debtor's employer to make deductions from his earnings and send these payments directly to you. You may attach wages, commissions and bonuses. You may not attach Social Security, old age pensions or disability pensions. Servicemen's pay may only be attached through the Ministry of Defence. You may attach wages of an owner of a limited company, but not that of a self-employed debtor, such as a proprietor or partner in a firm.

Attachment of earnings results in payment if the debtor has secure employment. If he changes jobs, you have to make a fresh application.

You may apply for an earnings attachment to the county court for the district in which the debtor resides. If this is not the court that issued the judgment, you must ask the judgment court to transfer the case to the County Court in the debtor's locality.

Your application for attachment of earnings is served on the debtor by the court. Within eight days of its receipt the debtor must complete and return to the court a form detailing his financial information. The court will then issue a provisional order stating the amount to be deducted from the debtor's earnings for each pay period. If you object, you may request a hearing before a court officer and present your reasons for a higher amount in person.

Highlight

A more direct way to collect is to have the court order the debtor's employer to make deductions from his earnings and send these payments directly to you.

CHAPTER 10

Once a final attachment order is entered the employer must obey it or face court sanctions. Where there is more than one creditor with an attachment on earnings, the earliest attachment is paid first.

Garnishee proceeding

A garnishee proceeding results in an order directed to a third party who holds money on behalf of, or owes money to, the debtor. It orders the third party to hold any such moneys until there is a court hearing to decide your claim. You may find that there are other people with claims against the debtor.

Who can you garnishee?

- Banks and building societies; only where an account is in the sole name of the debtor
- Solicitors; they often hold money on behalf of their clients.
- Tenants who pay rent to the debtor.
- Employers; only where money is actually due, not where merely accruing (see 'Attachment of earnings'). It would be more appropriate to use a garnishee where you expect a single week's or month's pay to cover the debt.

Each garnishee order works only once. It operates at the precise moment it is served on the garnishee. If at that moment the garnishee does not owe the debtor money, you will be unsuccessful.

The garnishee is permitted to pay out any money that has a prior call. For example, if you garnishee a bank and the debtor has written out a cheque to someone the day before you serve the garnishee and it is in the clearing system, it will be paid despite your order.

Finally, remember that a garnishee will be effective only if you maintain the element of surprise. Do not give any warning to the debtor that you intend to seek a garnishee, or he may simply remove the funds.

To apply for a garnishee you must send the court:

- an *Affidavit in Support of Application for Garnishee Order Form N349* (see page 86 for an example)
- the appropriate fee

The affidavit must state who you wish to garnishee and details of any bank account. If you have details of the bank and not of the account, the bank will, for a fee, search its records for the appropriate account. Check to see if you have any old cheques written by the debtor. This will show all relevant details.

Highlight

Finally, remember that a garnishee will be effective only if you maintain the element of surprise.

If the court grants the application for a garnishee (known as an *Order Nisi*), the court will set a hearing date for the judge to decide how any money held by the garnishee is to be dealt with. All other claims on the money will be settled here.

Charging order

A charging order gives you a legal charge over the debtor's title to a property or shares in a company. This means the debtor cannot sell the property without paying you first. Whilst a charging order does not provide you with actual payment, it does provide good security and is probably the most effective method of enforcing a judgment.

To obtain a charging order, you first have to know whether the debtor owns any property or shares.

If you know his address you can search the Land Registry to see if he owns the property. The Land Registers are open to the public; a search currently costs £4. Contact any Land Registry (head office tel: 0171 917 8888).

There is no way of doing a central search for ownership of shares in limited companies. You can, however, search at Companies House to see if the debtor is a director of a company. If he is, he may own shares in it and this can be checked at Companies House (tel: 01222 388588).

To apply for a charging order, send the court an affidavit containing the following:

1. the name and address of the debtor and any known creditors
2. the amount outstanding on the judgment
3. the identity of the asset to be charged, i.e. the details of the property and title number
4. the reason for your belief that the debtor owns the asset, i.e. refer to the land registry title
5. the appropriate fee

As with a garnishee, the court will, if it grants the order, list a hearing date to determine the matter more fully. The court grants a *Charging Order Nisi* and, after the hearing, a *Charging Order Absolute*.

You can protect your order by entering a 'caution' against the registered title. To do so contact the Land Registry.

Highlight

Whilst a charging order does not provide you with actual payment, it does provide good security and is probably the most effective method of enforcing a judgment.

Useful strategies

Before you decide which collection method to use, you need to know as much as possible about the debtor's financial means.

Oral examination

To assist you, the court can compel the debtor to come to court and answer questions under oath concerning his finances and ability to pay the judgment. This is called an oral examination.

Oral examinations are most effective as a simple way of notifying the debtor that you mean business and will not let the matter rest. But oral examinations may be of little use in extracting information that you can act on. Generally if your debtor has the money to pay you, he will do so after a few reminders. If he does not, it is likely he will seek to avoid you altogether, in which case he will be unwilling to attend an oral examination. If he does attend, he may not give you answers that help you.

If a debtor fails to attend an appointment for an oral examination, the court may issue a warrant for the debtor's arrest.

To request an oral examination of the debtor you should apply to the court jurisdiction where the debtor resides or conducts business. You must complete a *Request for Oral Examination Form N316* (see page 85) and return it to the court with your fee. The court will issue an order requiring the debtor to appear in court for an oral examination. The court will also notify you of the date.

You may request the debtor bring documents with him to the hearing to provide details about his means, i.e. pay slips or accounts if he is self-employed or bank statements.

At the oral examination you may directly question the debtor or request that the examination be conducted by the court officer. Some typical questions include:

1. What assets do you own?
2. Are you owed any money? If so, by whom?
3. Do you have a job? If so, where? What is your pay?
4. Do you have a bank account? If so, where? What is the account number?

5. Do you rent or own your house or flat? If you own, how is title held? What is the title number if registered? What is the value of the property? What is owed on the mortgage?

6. What other income do you have? Do you own any shares?

7. Does your spouse have a job? Where? On what salary?

8. What other debts do you have? Are there other wage attachments, warrants or garnishes against you?

These are illustrative. You can ask any reasonable questions to assist you in discovering how to best collect from the debtor.

You should always ask if the debtor wishes to prepare a payment plan. If the debtor proposes one acceptable to you, ask the court to enter it as an order. If the proposed plan is not acceptable, you at least have the information you need to decide how and whether to proceed against the debtor.

Enquiry agents

You can instruct a private firm of enquiry agents to find out information about a person or a business.

Enquiry agents have access to information not readily available to the general public. They also know where to look for more information. However, success cannot be guaranteed and the cost of employing an agent may not be worthwhile. In the case of companies and businesses, there is a lot of information available if you know where to look. The bigger the company, the more information will be available.

In the case of limited companies you can search at Companies House and obtain the registered office of the company, a list of its directors and possibly its recent accounts.

Highlight

Enquiry agents have access to information not readily available to the general public.

Bankruptcy/winding up proceedings

Another option open to you if your judgment remains unpaid is to commence bankruptcy/winding up proceedings. These can be used to exert pressure on a debtor in the hope he will then pay voluntarily.

There are two types of proceedings that can be used. The terminology is different in the case of limited companies, but the effects are the same whether it is a company, a business or an individual.

Statutory demand

A statutory demand is a formal demand for payment and is the first step in bankruptcy proceedings. It must be on the standard form, available from legal stationers, and cannot be used in cases where the sum owed is less than £750. It must be served personally on the debtor.

Once served, the debtor has three weeks in which to pay. If the debtor fails to do so, you are then at liberty to issue bankruptcy proceedings in the appropriate court.

The real benefit of statutory demands, if your claim is over the £750 limit, is that they do not have to be issued by the court, so there is no fee involved. You can simply fill out the standard form and serve it. It is an official-looking document and tends to attract response, particularly in the case of limited companies.

However, be very careful not to claim anything that is not strictly due. If the debtor disputes the demand, the debtor may issue proceedings in the County Court to have it set aside. If the debtor is successful, you may have to pay the costs of legal proceedings.

Bankruptcy/insolvency proceedings

This involves using court proceedings to have the debtor declared bankrupt. It is rarely an effective means of obtaining payment and has the added drawback that, as well as the court issue fee, you have to lodge a deposit of £300 for the receiver which is rarely recoverable. It is an action of last resort and should only be considered if you intend to see it through to the bitter end.

Highlight

It is an official-looking document and tends to attract response, particularly in the case of limited companies.

LAW PACK GUIDE

Glossary
of useful terms

A-D

Adjournment — the postponement to a subsequent date of an action pending in a court.

Affidavit — *see* **Statement of Truth**.

Allocation Questionnaire — Form to be sent to the court giving details of the nature of the action, from which the court allocate the case to one of the three tracks.

Appeal — the act of taking your claim, once a judgment is made at the lower court, to the next higher court to try to have it overturned, or to have a new decision on it.

Application — a request for an interlocutory order.

Arbitration — the determination of the dispute by the court, trade association or independent person as a third party.

Attachment of earnings order — used after a judgment is received. The creditor can use this to deduct a percentage of the debtor's wages for a certain time period or until the judgment is paid off.

Charging order — order over defendant's property to secure the amount of the judgment.

Civil action — a claim for money owed or property damage which proceeds in the civil courts, e.g. any County Court. All small claims are civil claims.

Civil Procedure Rules (CPR) — new code by which civil courts operate introduced 26th April 1999 and which unified and replaced High and County Court Rules formerly known as the White and Green Books, respectively.

Claim — a demand that someone owes you money or property.

Claim Form — the first document filed with the court in a Small Claims Track. This document will typically list the claimant and defendant, the reason the claimant is suing, and the amount. The court issues the claim form.

C-I

Claimant — the person doing the suing; formerly called the 'plaintiff'.

Contempt — a proceeding or an order from the judge saying that an individual has not followed the judge's orders. A criminal charge that may have serious consequences, i.e. jail.

Creditor — the claimant; an individual who is owed money by another.

Damages — a sum of money awarded by a court for a breach of contract or to remedy a wrong caused by the other party.

Debtor — i.e., the defendant. The individual who owes money to someone else.

Defendant — the individual who is being sued.

Default judgment — judgment entered when a defendant fails to answer a summons.

Demand letter — a letter sent by a creditor to the debtor requesting payment on the debt.

District Judge — a judge appointed to supervise the interlocutory and post-judgment stages of the case who can also try cases within a certain financial limit.

Extension of time — the judge may grant additional time to either side so that they have more time to prepare their case or lodge documents.

Fast Track — for cases with a financial range of £5,000 to £15,000. Limited legal costs are recoverable and a final hearing, which should be no more than one day, is to take place within 30 weeks of allocation.

Final hearing — the hearing where each side puts the detail of its case and the court makes a decision.

Fixed costs —the limited costs that can be obtained on a successful action under the small claims track.

Garnishee — the act of taking money held for a debtor toward payment of a judgment, i.e. from bank or building society accounts.

Injury — how you have been wronged; what it is that has been broken and needs to be fixed. *See also* **Damages**.

Interlocutory proceedings — the preliminary stages in civil proceedings occurring between the issue of the claim form and the trial, or final hearing.

I-P

Issuing fee — the amount you have to pay the court in order to start the proceedings. You must pay the fee when you file the lawsuit.

Judgment — the decision of the court in a matter before it.

Jurisdiction — whether the court has the power or ability to hear a particular dispute. This depends on many things, including the type of dispute, the amount contested, where the dispute arose, and the citizenship of the parties.

Liability — whether someone actually owes you money under the law, for their actions or nonactions.

Limitation period — the period allowed by statute in which a claim must be begun. It is six years for most cases but only three for personal injury. Time runs from when the cause of action arises i.e. when a debt becomes due or the date of an accident.

Lists — order of priority of cases awaiting trial with their expected start dates. A case enters the list after certain preliminary matters have been settled.

Litigation friend — the person who conducts proceedings on behalf of a child or patient subject to the Mental Health Act 1983. Usually a parent, but can be anyone appointed by the Court.

Mediation — this is where the parties seek assistance from a mediator to help them agree a settlement. It differs from arbitration in that no decision is made in favour of one party and both sides must agree to it. Some County Courts are now operating such schemes which are very cost effective.

Multi Track — all other cases which are not suitable for the Small Claims or Fast Track. Legal costs are recoverable.

Negligence — when the actions of someone are wrong in the eyes of the law.

Oral examination — procedure for defendant to give details of his financial circumstances to an officer of the court after judgment.

Order — an order by the judge directing either party to do something, i.e., lodge papers.

Overriding Objective — Rule 1.1 of the new Civil Procedure Rules which says the court is to deal with cases justly and which introduced the concept of proportionality taking into account the amount, importance and complexity of the issues and the financial position of each party.

Personal property — any property other than real estate.

P-W

Plaintiff — *see* **Claimant**.

Pleading — another name for the documents filed with the court setting out the claim or defence.

Preliminary hearing — a hearing where the court can give directions beyond the standard ones. Only used where special circumstances arise in the matter.

Secured debt — any obligation guaranteed by collateral of either property or personal property.

Service of process — the act of delivering the Court documents to the other party in the action.

Statement of truth — the allegations of the claimant against the defendant and the relief being claimed, i.e. damages; formerly called an 'affidavit'.

Small Claims Track — a special procedure in the County Court which deals exclusively with small civil actions, below £5,000.

Statement of case — the allegations of the claimant against the defendant and the relief being claimed, i.e. damages.

Statute of limitation — the time period allowed by the government as to the maximum time allowed between the time a debtor fails to pay you money and the time you sue the debtor. Three years with personal injuries, six years with contracts and property damage.

Tort — a civil wrong or injury.

Track — all cases are now allocated to one of the three tracks: Small Claims, Fast and Multi.

Trial — a more formal hearing than the final hearing in a Small Claims Track matter. You will be expected to have your witnesses, testimony and other evidence in order for this Court appearance.

Unsecured debt — an obligation not guaranteed by any form of collateral.

Witness summons — summons requiring a witness to attend court to give evidence or produce document. Failure to do so is contempt of court.

Warrant of execution — method of requesting court bailiff to enforce judgment. by seizing the debtor's goods.

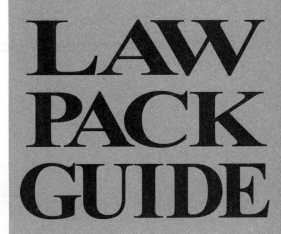

The forms
in this guide

This guide contains completed examples of the following Small Claim forms for reference. You should obtain copies of the relevant forms from your local County Court, or from the government Court Service web site at **www.courtservice.gov.uk**.

Other forms mentioned in this Guide are not included below because they are computer generated by the court and are case-specific.

Completed example of Claim Form N1

Claim Form

In the	
Claim No.	

Claimant

JOHN SMITH
1 THE HIGH STREET
LONDON
W1

SEAL

Defendant(s)

JAMES SHERBERT
14 SKINNER HOUSE
WALTHAM ROAD
LONDON
SE2 7BX

Brief details of claim

UNPAID INVOICE

Value

£579.97

Defendant's name and address

James Sherbert
14 Skinner House
Waltham Road
London
SE2 7BX

	£
Amount claimed	509.97
Court fee	70.00
Solicitor's costs	–
Total amount	579.97
Issue date	

The court office at

is open between 10 am and 4 pm Monday to Friday. When corresponding with the court, please address forms or letters to the Court Manager and quote the claim number.

Reproduced by Law Pack Publishing with the permission of the Controller of HMSO

N1 Claim form (CPR Part 7) (4.99)

(Continued on next page)

Completed example of Claim Form N1 (continued)

Claim No.

Particulars of Claim (attached)(to follow)

THE CLAIMANT CLAIMS THE SUM OF £500.00 BEING DUE BY THE DEFENDANT UNDER AN INVOICE DATED THE 25TH FEBRUARY 1999 NUMBER 5578 FOR GOODS SUPPLIED TO THE DEFENDANT AT HIS REQUEST BY THE CLAIMANT WHICH SUM REMAINS UNPAID.

THE CLAIMANT ALSO CLAIMS INTEREST IN ACCORDANCE WITH S.69 OF THE COUNTY COURTS ACT 1984 AT THE RATE OF 8% PER ANNUM FROM 25/2/99 TO THE DATE HEREOF BEING £9.97 AND CONTINUING AT THE DAILY RATE OF £0.11 UNTIL JUDGMENT OR SOONER PAYMENT.

Statement of Truth
*(I believe)(The Claimant believes) that the facts stated in these particulars of claim are true.
* I am duly authorised by the claimant to sign this statement

Full name ___ John Smith ___

Name of claimant's solicitor's firm ___

position or office held ___

signed ___ *John Smith* ___ (if signing on behalf of firm or company)
*(Claimant)(Litigation friend)(Claimant's solicitor)

*delete as appropriate

Claimant's or claimant's solicitor's address to which documents or payments should be sent if different from overleaf including (if appropriate) details of DX, fax or e-mail.

67

Example Notes for Claimant Form N1A

Notes for claimant on completing a claim form

Further information may be obtained from the court in a series of free leaflets.

- Please read all of these guidance notes before you begin completing the claim form. The notes follow the order in which information is required on the form.
- Court staff can help you fill in the claim form and give information about procedure once it has been issued. But they cannot give legal advice. If you need legal advice, for example, about the likely success of your claim or the evidence you need to prove it, you should contact a solicitor or a Citizens Advice Bureau.
- If you are filling in the claim form by hand, please use black ink and write in block capitals.
- Copy the completed claim form and the defendant's notes for guidance so that you have one copy for yourself, one copy for the court and one copy for each defendant. Send or take the forms to the court office with the appropriate fee. The court will tell you how much this is.

Notes on completing the claim form

Heading

You must fill in the heading of the form to indicate whether you want the claim to be issued in a county court or in the High Court (The High Court means either a District Registry (attached to a county court) or the Royal Courts of Justice in London). There are restrictions on claims which may be issued in the High Court (see 'Value' overleaf).

Use whichever of the following is appropriate:

'In the ....County Court'
(inserting the name of the court)

or

'In the High Court of Justice.......................Division'
(inserting eg. 'Queen's Bench' or 'Chancery' as appropriate)
'.............................District Registry'
(inserting the name of the District Registry)

or

'In the High Court of Justice.......................Division,
(inserting eg. 'Queen's Bench' or 'Chancery' as appropriate)
Royal Courts of Justice'

Claimant and defendant details

As the person issuing the claim, you are called the 'claimant'; the person you are suing is called the 'defendant'. Claimants who are under 18 years old (unless otherwise permitted by the court) and patients within the meaning of the Mental Health Act 1983, must have a litigation friend to issue and conduct court proceedings on their behalf. Court staff will tell you more about what you need to do if this applies to you.

You must provide the following information about yourself and the defendant according to the capacity in which you are suing and in which the defendant is being sued.

When suing or being sued as:-

an individual:

All known forenames and surname, whether Mr, Mrs, Miss, Ms or Other (e.g. Dr) and residential address (**including** postcode and telephone number) in England and Wales. Where the defendant is a proprietor of a business, a partner in a firm or an individual sued in the name of a club or other unincorporated association, the address for service should be the usual or last known place of residence **or** principal place of business of the company, firm or club or other unincorporated association.

Where the individual is:

under 18 write '(a child by Mr Joe Bloggs his litigation friend)' after the name. If the child is conducting proceedings on their own behalf write '(a child)' after the child's name.

a patient within the meaning of the Mental Health Act 1983 write '(by Mr Joe Bloggs his litigation friend)' after the patient's name.

trading under another name

you must add the words 'trading as' and the trading name e.g. 'Mr John Smith trading as Smith's Groceries'.

suing or being sued in a representative capacity

you must say what that capacity is e.g. 'Mr Joe Bloggs as the representative of Mrs Sharon Bloggs (deceased)'.

suing or being sued in the name of a club or other unincorporated association

add the words 'suing/sued on behalf of' followed by the name of the club or other unincorporated association.

a firm

enter the name of the firm followed by the words 'a firm' e.g. 'Bandbox - a firm' and an address for service which is either a partner's residential address or the principal or last known place of business.

a corporation (other than a company)

enter the full name of the corporation and the address which is either its principal office or any other place where the corporation carries on activities and which has a real connection with the claim.

a company registered in England and Wales

enter the name of the company and an address which is either the company's registered office or any place of business that has a real, or the most, connection with the claim e.g. the shop where the goods were bought.

an overseas company (defined by s744 of the Companies Act 1985)

enter the name of the company and either the address registered under s691 of the Act **or** the address of the place of business having a real, or the most, connection with the claim.

Reproduced by Law Pack Publishing with the permission of the Controller of HMSO

N1A Notes for claimant (4.99)

(Continued on next page)

Example Notes for Claimant Form N1A (continued)

Brief details of claim

Note: The facts and full details about your claim and whether or not you are claiming interest, should be set out in the 'particulars of claim' *(see note under 'Particulars of Claim').*

You must set out under this heading:

- a concise statement of the nature of your claim
- the remedy you are seeking e.g. payment of money; an order for return of goods or their value; an order to prevent a person doing an act; damages for personal injuries.

Value

If you are claiming a **fixed amount of money** (a 'specified amount') write the amount in the box at the bottom right-hand corner of the claim form against 'amount claimed'.

If you are not claiming a fixed amount of money (an 'unspecified amount') under 'Value' write "I expect to recover" followed by whichever of the following applies to your claim:

- "not more than £5,000" **or**
- "more than £5,000 but not more than £15,000" **or**
- "more than £15,000"

If you are **not able** to put a value on your claim, write "I cannot say how much I expect to recover".

Personal injuries

If your claim is for 'not more than £5,000' and includes a claim for personal injuries, you must also write "My claim includes a claim for personal injuries and the amount I expect to recover as damages for pain, suffering and loss of amenity is" followed by either:

- "not more than £1,000" **or**
- "more than £1,000"

Housing disrepair

If your claim is for 'not more than £5,000' and includes a claim for housing disrepair relating to residential premises, you must also write "My claim includes a claim against my landlord for housing disrepair relating to residential premises. The cost of the repairs or other work is estimated to be" followed by either:

- "not more than £1,000" **or**
- "more than £1,000"

If within this claim, you are making a claim for other damages, you must also write:

"I expect to recover as damages" followed by either:

- "not more than £1,000" **or**
- "more than £1,000"

Issuing in the High Court

You may only issue in the High Court if one of the following statements applies to your claim:-

"By law, my claim must be issued in the High Court. The Act which provides this is ....(specify Act)"

or

"I expect to recover more than £15,000"

or

"My claim includes a claim for personal injuries and the value of the claim is £50,000 or more"

or

"My claim needs to be in a specialist High Court list, namely...............................(state which list)".

If one of the statements does apply and you wish to, or must by law, issue your claim in the High Court, write the words "I wish my claim to issue in the High Court because" followed by the relevant statement e.g. "I wish my claim to issue in the High Court because my claim includes a claim for personal injuries and the value of my claim is £50,000 or more."

Defendant's name and address

Enter in this box the full names and address of the defendant receiving the claim form (ie. one claim form for each defendant). If the defendant is to be served outside England and Wales, you may need to obtain the court's permission.

Particulars of claim

You may include your particulars of claim on the claim form in the space provided or in a separate document which you should head 'Particulars of Claim'. It should include the names of the parties, the court, the claim number and your address for service and also contain a statement of truth. You should keep a copy for yourself, provide one for the court and one for each defendant

Separate particulars of claim can either be served

- with the claim form **or**
- within 14 days after the date on which the claim form was served.

If your particulars of claim are served separately from the claim form, they must be served with the forms on which the defendant may reply to your claim.

Your particulars of claim must include

- a concise statement of the facts on which you rely
- a statement (if applicable) to the effect that you are seeking aggravated damages or exemplary damages
- details of any interest which you are claiming
- any other matters required for your type of claim as set out in the relevant practice direction

Address for documents

Insert in this box the address at which you wish to receive documents and/or payments, if different from the address you have already given under the heading 'Claimant'. The address must be in England or Wales. If you are willing to accept service by DX, fax or e-mail, add details.

Statement of truth

This must be signed by you, by your solicitor or your litigation friend, as appropriate.

Where the claimant is a registered company or a corporation the claim must be signed by either the director, treasurer, secretary, chief executive, manager or other officer of the company or (in the case of a corporation) the mayor, chairman, president or town clerk.

Completed example of Certificate of Service Form N215

Certificate of service

In the	CENTRAL LONDON COUNTY COURT
Claim No.	99 12345
Claimant	JOHN SMITH
Defendant	JAMES SHERBERT

On the 28th May 1999 ....(insert date)

the .... (insert title or description of documents served)

Claim Form

a copy of which is attached to this notice was served on (insert name of person served, including position i.e. partner, director if appropriate)

James Sherbert

Tick as appropriate

☐ by Document Exchange

☐ by first class post

☑ by delivering to or leaving

☐ by handing it to or leaving it with

☐ by fax machine (.................time sent)
(you may want to enclose a copy of the transmission sheet)

☐ by e-mail

☐ by other means (please specify)

at (insert address where service effected, include fax or DX number or e-mail address)

14 SKINNER HOUSE
WALTHAM ROAD
LONDON SE2 7BX

being the defendant's:

☐ registered office

☑ residence

☐ other (please specify)

☐ place of business

The date of service is therefore deemed to be .... 29th May 1999 .... (insert date - see over for guidance)

I confirm that at the time of signing this Certificate the document has not been returned to me as undelivered.

Signed *John Smith*

(Claimant)~~(Defendant)(Claimant's solicitor)(Defendant's solicitor)~~

Position or office held
(if signing on behalf of firm or company)

Date 28th May 1999

Reproduced by Law Pack Publishing with the permission of the Controller of HMSO

N215 - w3 Certificate of service (4.99)

Completed example of Response Pack Form N9

Response Pack

You should read the 'notes for defendant' attached to the claim form which will tell you when and where to send the forms

Included in this pack are:
- either **Admission Form N9A** (if the claim is for a specified amount) or **Admission Form N9C** (if the claim is for an unspecified amount or is not a claim for money)
- either **Defence and Counterclaim Form N9B** (if the claim is for a specified amount) or **Defence and Counterclaim Form N9D** (if the claim is for an unspecified amount or is not a claim for money)
- **Acknowledgment of service** (see below)

If you admit the claim or the amount claimed and/or you want time to pay	► **Complete** the admission form
If you admit part of the claim	► the admission form and the defence form
If you dispute the whole claim or wish to make a claim (a counterclaim) against the claimant	► the defence form
If you need 28 days (rather than 14) from the date of service to prepare your defence, or wish to contest the court's jurisdiction	► the acknowledgment of service
If you do nothing, judgment may be entered against you	

Acknowledgment of Service

Defendant's full name if different from the name given on the claim form

....

....

In the	CENTRAL LONDON COUNTY COURT
Claim No.	99 12345
Claimant (including ref.)	JOHN SMITH (JS/as)
Defendant	JAMES SHERBERT

Address to which documents about this claim should be sent (including reference if appropriate)

JAMES SHERBERT
14 SKINNER HOUSE
WALTHAM ROAD
LONDON

Postcode SE2 7BX

Tel. no. 0171 123 4567

	if applicable
fax no.	
DX no.	
e-mail	

If you file an acknowledgment of service but do not file a defence within 28 days of the date of service of the claim form, or particulars of claim if served separately, judgment may be entered against you.

If you do not file an application within 28 days of the date of service of the claim form, or particulars of claim if served separately, it will be assumed that you accept the court's jurisdiction and judgment may be entered against you.

Tick the appropriate box

1. I intend to defend all of this claim ✓
2. I intend to defend part of this claim ☐
3. I intend to contest jurisdiction ☐

Date 15/5/99

Signed *James Sherbert*

(Defendant)(Defendant's solicitor)
(Litigation friend)

Position or office held (if signing on behalf of firm or company)

The court office at

is open between 10 am and 4 pm Monday to Friday. When corresponding with the court, please address forms or letters to the Court Manager and quote the claim number.

N9 Response Pack (4.99)

Completed example of Response Pack Form of Admission N9A

Admission (specified amount)

- You have a limited number of days to complete and return this form
- Before completing this form, please read the notes for guidance attached to the claim form

When to fill in this form
- Only fill in this form if you are admitting all or some of the claim **and** you are asking for time to pay

How to fill in this form
- Tick the correct boxes and give as much information as you can. **Then sign and date the form.** If necessary provide details on a separate sheet, add the claim number and attach it to this form.
- Make your offer of payment in box 11 on the back of this form. **If you make no offer the claimant will decide how much and when you should pay.**
- If you are not an individual, you should ensure that you provide sufficient details about the assets and liabilities of your firm, company or corporation to support any offer of payment made in box 11.
- You can get help to complete this form at **any** county court office or Citizens Advice Bureau.

Where to send this form
- **If you admit the claim in full**
  Send the completed form to the address shown on the claim form as one to which documents should be sent.
- **If you admit only part of the claim**
  Send the form **to the court** at the address given on the claim form, together with the defence form (N9B).

How much of the claim do you admit?
- [✓] I admit the full amount claimed as shown on the claim form   **or**
- [ ] I admit the amount of   £

1 Personal details

Surname	SHERBERT
Forename	JAMES

[✓] Mr [ ] Mrs [ ] Miss [ ] Ms
[✓] Married [ ] Single [ ] Other (specify)

Age 40

Address 14 SKINNER HOUSE
WALTHAM ROAD
LONDON

Postcode SE2 7BX

Tel. no. 0171 123 4567

In the	CENTRAL LONDON COUNTY COURT
Claim No.	99 12345
Claimant (including ref.)	JOHN SMITH (JS/as)
Defendant	JAMES SHERBERT

2 Dependants *(people you look after financially)*

Number of children in each age group

Under 11 [ ]   11-15 [ ]   16-17 [ ]   18 & over [ ]

Other dependants *(give details)*   WIFE

3 Employment

- [ ] **I am employed as a**
  My employer is

  Jobs other than main job *(give details)*

- [✓] **I am self employed as a**   ELECTRICIAN   £16,000
  Annual turnover is ....

  - [ ] **I am not** in arrears with my national insurance contributions, income tax and VAT

  - [ ] **I am** in arrears and I owe .... £

  Give details of:
  (a) contracts and other work in hand   VARIES FROM WEEK TO WEEK
  (b) any sums due for work done   NONE

- [ ] **I have been unemployed for**   years   months

- [ ] **I have been unemployed for**
- [ ] **I am a pensioner**

4 Bank account and savings

- [✓] **I have a bank account**
  - [✓] The account is in credit by £350.00
  - [ ] The account is overdrawn by ...   £

- [ ] **I have a savings or building society account**
  The amount in the account is ......   £

5 Residence

I live in
[ ] my own house   [ ] lodgings
[ ] my jointly owned house   [✓] council accommodation
[ ] rented accommodation

Reproduced by Law Pack Publishing with the permission of the Controller of HMSO

N9A Form of admission (specified amount) (4.99)

(Continued on next page)

Completed example of Response Pack Form of Admission N9A (continued)

6 Income

My usual take home pay (including overtime, commission, bonuses etc)	£ 220	per wk
	£ —	per
Income support	£ —	per
Child benefit(s)	£ —	per
Other state benefit(s)	£ —	per
My pension(s)	£ —	per
Others living in my home give me		
Other income (give details below)		
	£ —	per
	£ —	per
	£ —	per
Total income	**£ 220**	**per wk**

7 Expenses

(*Do not* include any payments made by other members of the household out of their own income)

I have regular expenses as follows:

	£ —	per
Mortgage (including second mortgage)	£ 25	per wk
Rent	£ 6	per wk
Council tax	£ 3	per wk
Gas	£ 5	per wk
Electricity	£ 2	per wk
Water charges		
TV rental and licence	£ 15	per wk
HP repayments	£ 28	per wk
Mail order	£ —	per
Housekeeping, food, school meals	£ 75	per wk
Travelling expenses	£ 15	per wk
Children's clothing	£ 5	per wk
Maintenance payments	£ —	per
Others (not court orders or credit debts listed in boxes 9 and 10)		
	£ —	per
	£ —	per
	£ —	per
Total expenses	**£179**	**per wk**

8 Priority debts

(This section is for arrears only. *Do not* include regular expenses listed in box 7.)

	£ —	per
	£ —	per
Rent arrears	£ —	per
Mortgage arrears	£ —	per
Council tax/Community Charge arrears	£ —	per
Water charges arrears	£ —	per
Fuel debts: Gas	£ —	per
Electricity	£ —	per
Other	£ —	per
Maintenance arrears		
Others (give details below)	£ —	per
	£ —	per
Total priority debts	**£ —**	**per**

9 Court orders

		£ per
Claim No.		
Court	N/A	
Total court order instalments	**£**	**per**

Of the payments above, I am behind with payments to (*please list*)

10 Credit debts

Loans and credit card devts (*please list*)	£	per
	£	per
N/A	£	per

Of the payments above, I am behind with payments to (*please list*)

11 Offer of payment

☐ I can pay the amount admitted on

or

☑ I can pay by monthly instalments of   £ 50.00

If you cannot pay immediately, please give brief reasons below

12 Declaration

I declare that the details I have given above are true to the best of my knowledge

Position or office held (if signing on behalf of firm or company)	N/A

Signed   *James Sherbert*

Date   15/6/99

Completed example of Defendant's Reply Form N9B (defence)

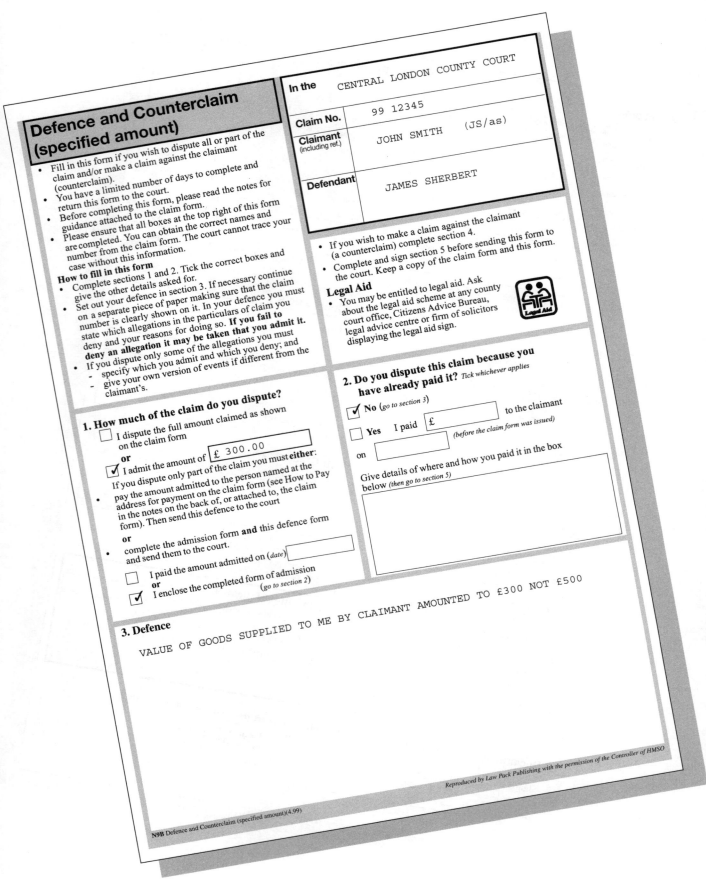

Defence and Counterclaim (specified amount)

- Fill in this form if you wish to dispute all or part of the claim and/or make a claim against the claimant (counterclaim).
- You have a limited number of days to complete and return this form to the court.
- Before completing this form, please read the notes for guidance attached to the claim form.
- Please ensure that all boxes at the top right of this form are completed. You can obtain the correct names and number from the claim form. The court cannot trace your case without this information.

How to fill in this form
- Complete sections 1 and 2. Tick the correct boxes and give the other details asked for.
- Set out your defence in section 3. If necessary continue on a separate piece of paper making sure that the claim number is clearly shown on it. In your defence you must state which allegations in the particulars of claim you deny and your reasons for doing so. **If you fail to deny an allegation it may be taken that you admit it.**
- If you dispute only some of the allegations you must
  - specify which you admit and which you deny; and
  - give your own version of events if different from the claimant's.

In the	CENTRAL LONDON COUNTY COURT
Claim No.	99 12345
Claimant (including ref.)	JOHN SMITH (JS/as)
Defendant	JAMES SHERBERT

- If you wish to make a claim against the claimant (a counterclaim) complete section 4.
- Complete and sign section 5 before sending this form to the court. Keep a copy of the claim form and this form.

Legal Aid
- You may be entitled to legal aid. Ask about the legal aid scheme at any county court office, Citizens Advice Bureau, legal advice centre or firm of solicitors displaying the legal aid sign.

1. How much of the claim do you dispute?

☐ I dispute the full amount claimed as shown on the claim form

or

☑ I admit the amount of £ 300.00

If you dispute only part of the claim you must **either**:
- pay the amount admitted to the person named at the address for payment on the claim form (see How to Pay in the notes on the back of, or attached to, the claim form). Then send this defence to the court

or

- complete the admission form **and** this defence form and send them to the court.

☐ I paid the amount admitted on (date)

or

☑ I enclose the completed form of admission *(go to section 2)*

2. Do you dispute this claim because you have already paid it? *Tick whichever applies*

☑ **No** *(go to section 3)*

☐ **Yes** I paid £ _____ to the claimant *(before the claim form was issued)*

on _____

Give details of where and how you paid it in the box below *(then go to section 5)*

3. Defence

VALUE OF GOODS SUPPLIED TO ME BY CLAIMANT AMOUNTED TO £300 NOT £500

Reproduced by Law Pack Publishing with the permission of the Controller of HMSO

N9B Defence and Counterclaim (specified amount)(4.99)

(Continued on next page)

Completed example of Defendant's Reply Form N9B (defence) (continued)

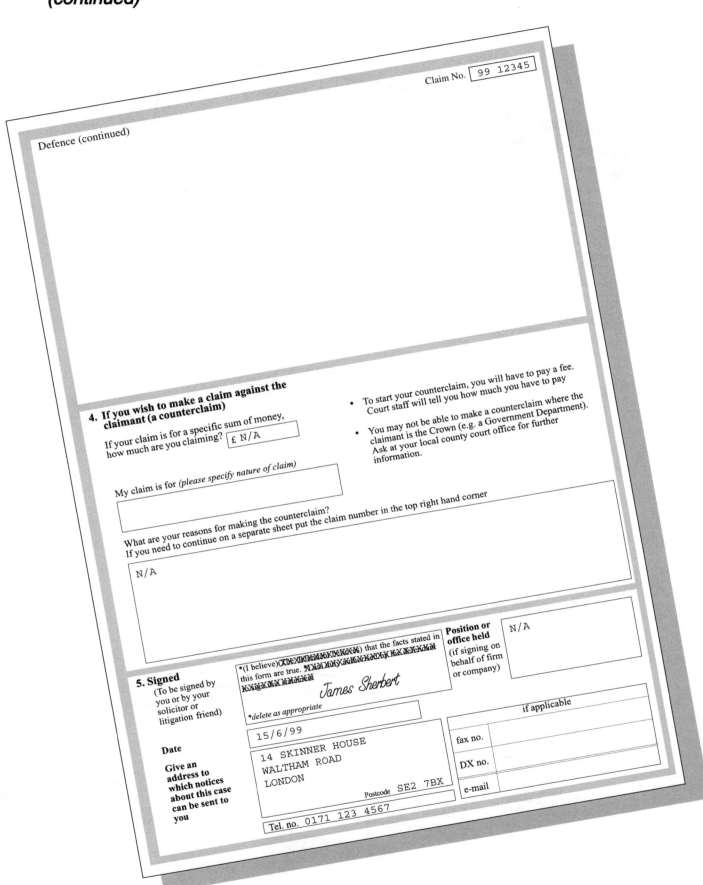

Claim No. | 99 12345

Defence (continued)

4. If you wish to make a claim against the claimant (a counterclaim)

If your claim is for a specific sum of money, how much are you claiming? £ N/A

- To start your counterclaim, you will have to pay a fee. Court staff will tell you how much you have to pay

- You may not be able to make a counterclaim where the claimant is the Crown (e.g. a Government Department). Ask at your local county court office for further information.

My claim is for (please specify nature of claim)

What are your reasons for making the counterclaim?
If you need to continue on a separate sheet put the claim number in the top right hand corner

N/A

Position or office held
(if signing on behalf of firm or company)   N/A

*(I believe)(XXXXXXXXXXXXXXXXXX) that the facts stated in this form are true. XXXXXXXXXXXXXXXXXXXXXXX XXXXXXXX XXXXXXX

James Sherbert

delete as appropriate

5. Signed
(To be signed by you or by your solicitor or litigation friend)

Date

Give an address to which notices about this case can be sent to you

15/6/99

14 SKINNER HOUSE
WALTHAM ROAD
LONDON
Postcode SE2 7BX

Tel. no. 0171 123 4567

if applicable

fax no.

DX no.

e-mail

Completed example of Request for Judgment Form and Reply to Admission Form N225

Request for judgment and reply to admission (specified amount)

- Tick box A or B. If you tick box B you must complete the details in that part and in part C. Make sure that all the case details are given. Remember to sign and date the form. Your signature certifies that the information you have given is correct.
- If the defendant has given an address on the form of admission to which correspondence should be sent, which is different from the address shown on the claim form, you must tell the court.
- Return the completed form to the court.

In the	CENTRAL LONDON COUNTY COURT
Claim No.	99 12345
Claimant (including ref)	James Sherbert JS/as
Defendant (including ref)	

A ☐ The defendant has not filed an admission or defence to my claim

Complete all the judgment details at C. Decide how and when you want the defendant to pay. You can ask for the judgment to be paid by instalments or in one payment.

B ☑ The defendant admits that all the money is owed

Tick only **one** box below and complete all the judgment details at C.

☑ **I accept the defendant's proposal for payment**

Say how the defendant intends to pay. The court will send the defendant an order to pay. You will also be sent a copy.

☐ **The defendant has not made any proposal for payment**

Say how you want the defendant to pay. You can ask for the judgment to be paid by instalments or in one payment. The court will send the defendant an order to pay. You will also be sent a copy.

☐ **I do NOT accept the defendant's proposal for payment**

Say how you want the defendant to pay. Give your reasons for objecting to the defendant's offer of payment in the space opposite. (Continue on the back of this form if necessary.) Send this form to the court **with defendant's admission N9A**. The court will fix a rate of payment and send the defendant an order to pay. You will also be sent a copy.

C Judgment details

I would like the judgment to be paid

☑ (immediately)

☐ (by instalments of £ [   ] per month)

☐ (in full by [   ])

Amount of claim as admitted (including interest at date of issue)	509	97
Interest since date of claim (if any). Period from 25/5/99 to 25/8/99	10	56
Rate 8 %	70	00
Court fees shown on claim		
Solicitor's costs (if any) on issuing claim	590	53
Sub Total	590	53
Solicitor's costs (if any) on entering judgment **Sub Total**	300	00
Deduct amount (if any) paid since issue		
Amount payable by defendant	290	53

I certify that the information given is correct

Signed *John Smith*

(Claimant)(XXXXXXXXXXXXXXXXXXXXXXXXXXX)

Date   30/8/99

Position or office held [   ]

(if signing on behalf of firm or company)

The court office at

is open between 10 am and 4 pm Monday to Friday. When corresponding with the court, please address forms and letters to the Court Manager and quote the Claim number

Reproduced by Law Pack Publishing with the permission of the Controller of HMSO

N225   Request for judgment and reply to admission (specified amount) (4.99)

Completed example of Allocation Questionnaire Form N150

Allocation questionnaire

In the	CENTRAL LONDON COUNTY COURT
Claim No.	99 12345
Last date for filing with court office	10 JUNE 1999

SEAL

To

JOHN SMITH

Please read the notes on page five before completing the questionnaire

Please note the date by which it must be returned and the name of the court it should be returned to since this may be different from the court where proceedings were issued.

If you have settled this case (or if you settle it on a future date) and do not need to have it heard or tried, you must let the court know immediately.

☐ Yes   ☑ No

A Settlement

Do you wish there to be a one month stay to attempt to settle the case?

B Track

Which track do you consider is most suitable for your case? *(Tick one box)*

☑ small claims   ☐ fast track   ☐ multi-track

If you think your case is suitable for a specialist list, say which:

If you have indicated a track which would not be the normal track for the case, please give brief reasons for your choice:

Reproduced by Law Pack Publishing with the permission of the Controller of HMSO

I

N150 Allocation questionnaire (4.99)

(Continued on next page)

Completed example of Allocation Questionnaire Form N150 (continued)

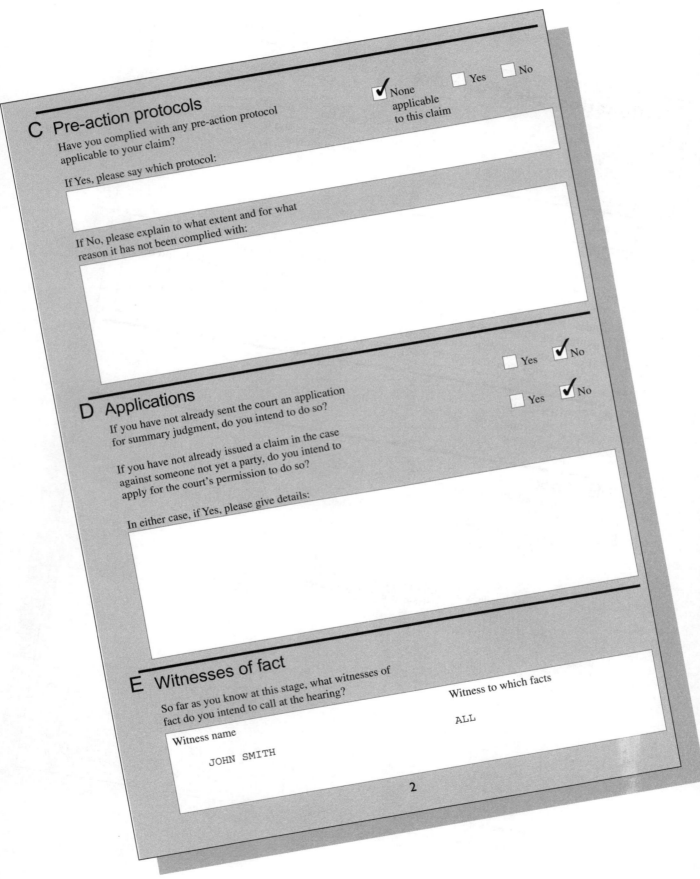

C Pre-action protocols

Have you complied with any pre-action protocol applicable to your claim?

☑ None applicable to this claim   ☐ Yes   ☐ No

If Yes, please say which protocol:

If No, please explain to what extent and for what reason it has not been complied with:

D Applications

If you have not already sent the court an application for summary judgment, do you intend to do so?

☐ Yes   ☑ No

If you have not already issued a claim in the case against someone not yet a party, do you intend to apply for the court's permission to do so?

☐ Yes   ☑ No

In either case, if Yes, please give details:

E Witnesses of fact

So far as you know at this stage, what witnesses of fact do you intend to call at the hearing?

Witness to which facts

ALL

Witness name

JOHN SMITH

2

(Continued on next page)

Completed example of Allocation Questionnaire Form N150 (continued)

F Experts' evidence

Do you wish to use expert evidence at the hearing? □ Yes ✓ No

Have you already copied any experts' report(s) to the other party(ies)? □ None obtained as yet

Please list the experts whose evidence you think you will use:

Field of expertise (eg. orthopaedic surgeon, mechanical engineer)

Expert's name

□ Yes □ No

Will you and the other party use the same expert(s)?

If No, please explain why not:

□ Yes □ No

Do you want your expert(s) to give evidence orally at the hearing or trial?

If Yes, give the reasons why you think oral evidence is necessary:

□ Yes ✓ No

G Location of trial

Is there any reason why your case needs to be heard at a particular court?

If Yes, give reasons (eg. particular facilities required, convenience of witnesses, etc.)

and specify the court:

3

(Continued on next page)

H Representation and estimate of hearing/trial time

☑ No ☐ Solicitor ☐ Counsel

Do you expect to be represented by a solicitor or counsel at the hearing/trial?

How long do you estimate it will take to put your case to the court at the hearing/trial?

| 1/2 days | hours | minutes |

If there are days when you, your representative, expert or an essential witness will not be able to attend court, give details:

Dates not available

Name

I Costs (only relates to costs incurred by legal representatives)

£ 140

What is your estimate of costs incurred to date, excluding disbursements, VAT and court fees?

£ 100

What do you estimate the overall costs are likely to be, excluding disbursements, VAT and court fees?

J Other information

☑ Yes ☐ No

Have you attached documents you wish the judge to take into account when allocating the case?

☑ Yes ☐ No

Have they been served on the other parties?

☐ Yes ☑ No

If yes, say when

Have the other parties agreed their content?

N/A ☐ Yes ☐ No

Have you attached a list of the directions you think appropriate for the management of your case?

☐ Yes ☐ No

Are they agreed with the other parties?

Are there any other facts which might affect the timetable the court will set? If so, please state

None

Date 28th May 1999

Signed *John Smith*

[Counsel][Solicitor for the][Claimant][Defendant]

4

(Continued on next page)

Notes for completing an allocation questionnaire

- If the case is not settled, a judge must allocate it to an appropriate case management track. To help the judge choose the most just and cost-effective track, you must now complete the attached questionnaire.
- If you fail to return the allocation questionnaire by the date given, the judge may make an order which leads to your claim or defence being struck out, or hold an allocation hearing. If there is an allocation hearing the judge may order any party who has not filed their questionnaire to pay, immediately, the costs of that hearing.
- If you wish to make an application, for example, for special directions, for summary judgment on the grounds that the other party has no reasonable chance of success in their claim or defence, or for permission to add another party to the claim, you should send it and any required fee with the completed allocation questionnaire. If a hearing is fixed for your application, it may also be used as an allocation hearing.
- Any other documents you wish the judge to take into account should be filed with the questionnaire. But you must confirm that the documents have been sent to the other party, or parties, saying when they would have received them and whether they agreed their contents.
- Use a separate sheet if you need more space for your answers marking clearly which section the information refers to. Write the case number on it, sign and date it and attach it securely to the questionnaire.
- The letters below refer to the sections of the questionnaire and tell you what information is needed.

A Settlement

If you think that you and the other party may be able to negotiate a settlement you should tick the 'Yes' box. The court may order a stay, whether or not all the other parties to the case agree. You should still complete the rest of the questionnaire, even if you are requesting a stay. Where a stay is granted it will be for an initial period of one month.

B Track

The basic guide by which cases are normally allocated to a track depends on the money value of the claim, although other factors such as the complexity of the case will also be considered:

Small Claims track	Claims valued at £5,000 or less unless they include a claim for personal injuries worth over £1,000; or a claim for housing disrepair where the costs of the repairs or other work is more than £1,000 and any other claim for damages is more than £1,000
Fast track	Claims valued at more than £5,000 but not more than £15,000
Multi-track	Claims over £15,000

A leaflet available from the court office explains these limits in greater detail.

C Pre-action protocols

For certain kinds of claim, there are protocols which set out what ought to be done before court proceedings are issued. As at April 1999 there are protocols for clinical negligence and personal injury claims.

D Applications

If you intend to apply for summary judgment or for permission to add another party to the claim or make any other application you should, if you have not already done so, file the application with your completed allocation questionnaire.

E Witnesses of fact

Remember to include yourself, if you will be giving evidence; but not experts, who should be included in section F.

F Experts' evidence

Oral or written expert evidence will only be allowed at the trial with the court's permission. The judge will decide what permission it seems appropriate to give when the case is allocated to track.

G Location of trial

High Court cases are usually heard at the Royal Courts of Justice or certain Civil Trial Centres. Other multi-track cases are heard at the Civil Trial Centre for the court where they are proceeding. Fast track cases are usually heard either at the Civil court in which they are proceeding or its Civil Trial Centre. The court office will tell you which is the Civil Trial Centre for any particular county court. Small claim cases are usually heard at the court in which they are proceeding.

H Representation and estimate of hearing/trial time

If the case is allocated to the fast track, no more than one day will be allowed for the trial of the whole case.

5

Completed example of Request for Warrant of Execution Form N323

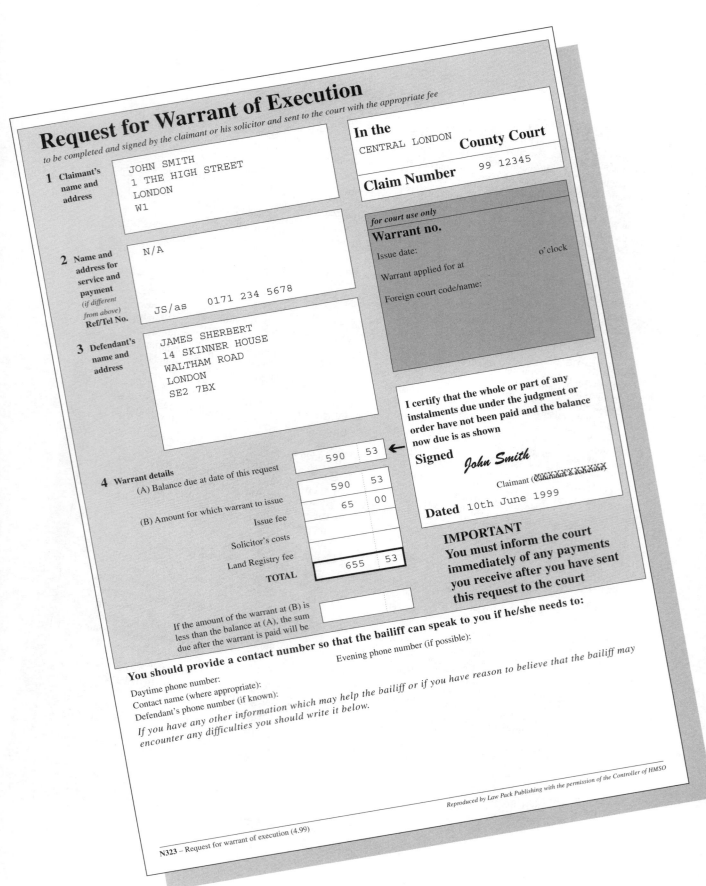

Request for Warrant of Execution

to be completed and signed by the claimant or his solicitor and sent to the court with the appropriate fee

1	Claimant's name and address	JOHN SMITH 1 THE HIGH STREET LONDON W1
2	Name and address for service and payment *(if different from above)* Ref/Tel No.	N/A JS/as 0171 234 5678
3	Defendant's name and address	JAMES SHERBERT 14 SKINNER HOUSE WALTHAM ROAD LONDON SE2 7BX

In the

CENTRAL LONDON **County Court**

Claim Number   99 12345

for court use only

Warrant no.

Issue date: o'clock

Warrant applied for at

Foreign court code/name:

I certify that the whole or part of any instalments due under the judgment or order have not been paid and the balance now due is as shown

Signed   *John Smith*

Claimant (Claimant's solicitor)

Dated 10th June 1999

4 Warrant details

(A) Balance due at date of this request	590	53
(B) Amount for which warrant to issue	590	53
Issue fee	65	00
Solicitor's costs		
Land Registry fee		
TOTAL	655	53

If the amount of the warrant at (B) is less than the balance at (A), the sum due after the warrant is paid will be

IMPORTANT
You must inform the court immediately of any payments you receive after you have sent this request to the court

You should provide a contact number so that the bailiff can speak to you if he/she needs to:

Daytime phone number: Evening phone number (if possible):

Contact name (where appropriate):

Defendant's phone number (if known):

If you have any other information which may help the bailiff or if you have reason to believe that the bailiff may encounter any difficulties you should write it below.

N323 – Request for warrant of execution (4.99)

Completed example of Application Notice N244

In the   CENTRAL LONDON

Claim no.   99 12345

Warrant no. (If applicable)

Claimant (including ref.)   JOHN SMITH   JS/as

Defendant(s) (including ref.)   JAMES SHERBERT

Date   1 JUNE 1999

Application Notice

- You must complete Parts A **and** B, **and** Part C if applicable
- Send any relevant fee and the completed application to the court with any draft order, witness statement or other evidence; and sufficient copies of these for service on each respondent

You should provide this information for listing the application

1. Do you wish to have your application dealt with at a hearing?

   Yes ☐   No ☐   If Yes, please complete 2

2. Time estimate ——— (hours) ——— (mins)

   Is this agreed by all parties? ☐ Yes   ☐ No

   Level of judge _____

3. Parties to be served:

(on behalf of) (the claimant) (the defendant)

Part A

1. Enter your full name, or name of solicitor

I (We)(1)   John Smith

2. State clearly what order you are seeking and if possible attach a draft

intend to apply for an order (a draft of which is attached) that(2) the Court review its decision regarding the defendant's payments

3. Briefly set out why you are seeking the order. Include the material facts on which you rely, identifying any rule or statutory provision

because(3) the defendant has a part-time job as a security officer which he did not reveal, and I believe he is therefore able to pay the whole sum immediately, or more quickly in larger instalments

Part B

I (We) wish to rely on: *tick one box*   my statement of case ☐

the attached (witness statement)(affidavit) ☐

evidence in Part C in support of my application ☑

4. If you are not already a party to the proceedings, you must provide an address for service of documents

Signed   *John Smith*

(Applicant)('s solicitor)('s litigation friend)

Position or office held (if signing on behalf of firm or company)

Address to which documents about this claim should be sent (including reference if appropriate)(4)   if applicable

1 THE HIGH STREET
LONDON

fax no.

DX no.

e-mail

Postcode   W1 1AB

Tel. no.   0171 123 4567

The court office at

is open from 10am to 4pm Monday to Friday. When corresponding with the court please address forms or letters to the Court Manager and quote the claim number.

N244 Application Notice (4.99)

(Continued on next page)

Completed example of Application Notice N244 (continued)

Claim No. | 99 12345

Part C

I (We) wish to rely on the following evidence in support of this application:

LETTER FROM THE DEFENDANT'S EMPLOYER CONFIRMING THAT HE HAS A
PART-TIME JOB WITH THEM.

Statement of Truth

*(I believe)(The applicant believes) that the facts stated in this application are true

Signed *John Smith*

(Applicant)(XXXXXXXXXXXXXXXXXXXXX)

Position or office held
(if signing on behalf of firm or company)

Date 1/6/99

*delete as appropriate

Completed example of Request for Oral Examination Form N316

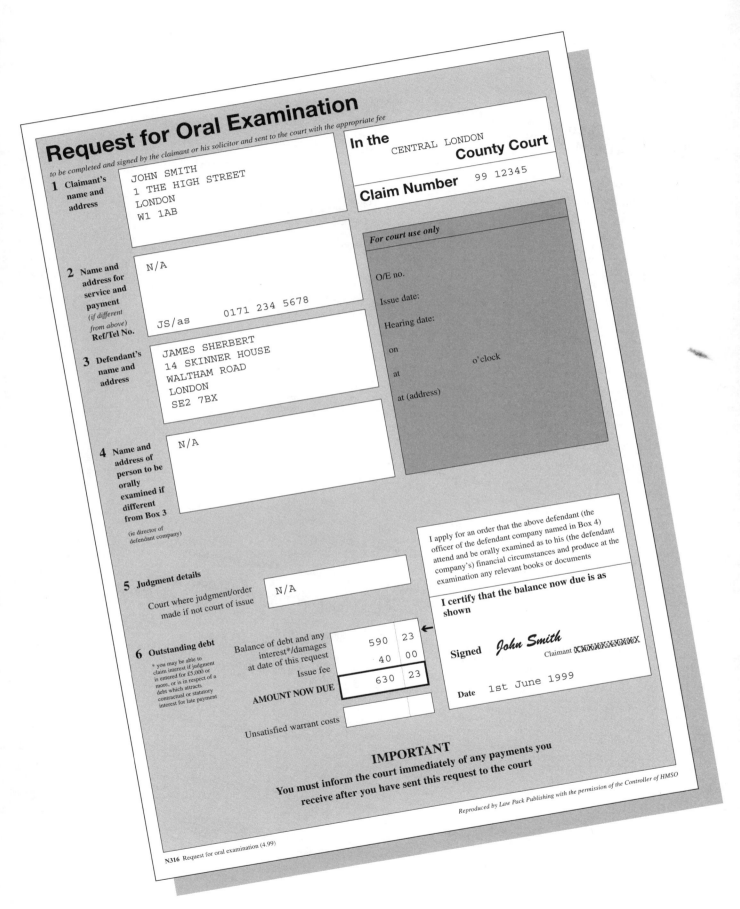

Request for Oral Examination

to be completed and signed by the claimant or his solicitor and sent to the court with the appropriate fee

In the CENTRAL LONDON **County Court**

Claim Number 99 12345

1 Claimant's name and address

JOHN SMITH
1 THE HIGH STREET
LONDON
W1 1AB

2 Name and address for service and payment
(if different from above)
Ref/Tel No.

N/A

JS/as   0171 234 5678

3 Defendant's name and address

JAMES SHERBERT
14 SKINNER HOUSE
WALTHAM ROAD
LONDON
SE2 7BX

For court use only

O/E no.

Issue date:

Hearing date:

on

at   o'clock

at (address)

4 Name and address of person to be orally examined if different from Box 3

(ie director of defendant company)

N/A

5 Judgment details

Court where judgment/order made if not court of issue

N/A

I apply for an order that the above defendant (the officer of the defendant company named in Box 4) attend and be orally examined as to his (the defendant company's) financial circumstances and produce at the examination any relevant books or documents

I certify that the balance now due is as shown

6 Outstanding debt

* you may be able to claim interest if judgment is entered for £5,000 or more, or is in respect of a debt which attracts contractual or statutory interest for late payment

Balance of debt and any interest*/damages at date of this request	590	23
Issue fee	40	00
AMOUNT NOW DUE	630	23
Unsatisfied warrant costs		

Signed *John Smith*   Claimant XXXXXXXXXXX

Date 1st June 1999

IMPORTANT

You must inform the court immediately of any payments you receive after you have sent this request to the court

Reproduced by Law Pack Publishing with the permission of the Controller of HMSO

N316 Request for oral examination (4.99)

Completed example of Affidavit for Garnishee Order Form N349

Sworn by (deponent) This is the (1st, 2nd etc) filed on behalf of (party) on (date filed)	on (date) affidavit by this deponent

Affidavit in support of Application for Garnishee Order Absolute

Claimant	John Smith
Defendant	James Sherbert
Garnishee	Barclays Bank plc

In the	CENTRAL LONDON	County Court
Claim No.	*always quote this*	99 12345
Claimant's Ref.		JS/as

I, *[Insert full name, address and occupation of deponent]*

John Smith, of The 1 High Street, London W1, Electrician

~~(SMKXXXX)~~ the above-named claimant, make oath and say:

1. That I ~~(XX)~~)
   on the 1st day June [199 9][20   ], obtained a judgment (or an order) in this court against
   the above-named defendant for the payment of the sum of £ for
   debt (or damages) and costs , including any interest to date *[where judgment is entered for more than
   £5000 or includes a sum in respect of contractural or late payment, the plaintiff may be entitled to further interest]* is still due and unpaid under the
   judgment (order)

2. That £ 590.53

3. That to the best of my information or belief the garnishee, National Bank plc
   of Head Office, 1 Royal Mint Court, London EC3) *[add if known]*
   is indebted to the defendent (in the sum of £ 600.00 *[state your grounds]*
   The reasons for my information and belief are:

   the defendant's replies at oral examination

4. That the garnishee is a deposit-taking institution having more than one place of business (and the name and address of the
   branch at which the defendant's account is believed to be held is:

   National Bank plc, Waltham Branch, 22 High Street, Waltham, London SE2) (~~XXXXXXXXXXXXX~~

   and the number of the account is believed to be 90980877 ~~XXXXXXXXXXXXXXXXXXXXXX~~ *[delete as appropriate]*
   ~~XXXXXXXXXXXXXXXXXXXXXXXXXXXXXXXXXXXX~~

5. That the last known address of the defendant is:

   14 Skinner House, Waltham Road, London SE2 7BX

Sworn at London in the
County of London
2nd day of June [199 9][20   ]

this }

Before me
Officer of a court, appointed by the Circuit Judge to take affidavits

This affidavit is filed on behalf of the claimant

Reproduced by Law Pack Publishing
with the permission of the Controller of HMSO

The court office at

is open between 10am and 4pm Monday to Friday. When corresponding with the court, please address forms and letters to the Court Manager and quote the claim number.

N349 Affidavit in support of application for garnishee order (Order 30, rule 2)(4.99)

LAW PACK GUIDE

Index

A-P

P-W

LAST WILL & TESTAMENT

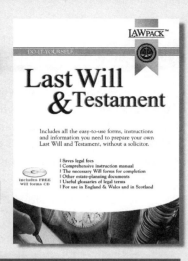

The Law Pack Will kit is the quick, economical and legally valid way to ensure your property goes to those whom you choose. This best-selling title includes an instruction manual and a choice of Will Forms for leaving the residue of an estate to adults and children. Valid in England & Wales and Scotland. Includes a free CD with Will Forms and other useful estate-organising documents.

Code P107 | ISBN 1 902646 22 3 | Sealed wallet | 307 x 217 mm | £9.99 | 2nd Edition

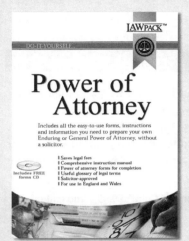

POWER OF ATTORNEY

With an increasingly elderly population, the demand for powers of attorney is growing. Creating a power of attorney is a straightforward procedure, but many people simply don't know how to do it or where to get the necessary forms. This new Kit includes an Enduring Power Attorney form and its registration documents and a General Power of Attorney, plus an instruction manual with background information. Free Forms CD included.

Code P104 | ISBN 1 902646 25 8 | Sealed wallet | 307 x 217 mm | £9.99 | 2nd Edition

RESIDENTIAL LETTING

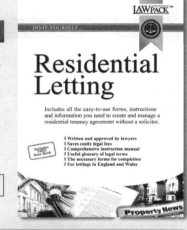

This Kit includes everything a residential landlord needs to let property. It contains an Assured Shorthold Tenancy agreement for letting the whole of a furnished or unfurnished house or flat, or for letting an individual room in a furnished or unfurnished house or flat shared with other tenants. An instruction manual covers the legal background, landlord's and tenant's obligations, rent control and gaining possession of your property. Also included are an Inventory and a Notice to Terminate, plus a free Rent Book.

Code P109 | ISBN 1 902646 73 8 | Sealed wallet | 307 x 217 mm | £9.99 | 4th Edition

LIMITED COMPANY

This Kit explains what a limited company is and provides all the documentation needed to set one up with a registered office in England, Wales or Scotland, at fraction of the cost of an 'off the shelf company'. It includes copies of the necessary Companies House forms, Memorandum of Association, Articles of Association, share certificates and an instruction manual which guides the reader step-by-step through the process and provides useful background information.

Code P101 | ISBN 1 902646 88 6 | Sealed wallet | 307 x 217 mm | £9.99 | 4th Edition

EMPLOYMENT CONTRACTS

This Kit contains all that an employer needs in order to prepare contracts for staff and so comply with legal requirements. Loose-leaf full- and part-time, temporary and domestic contracts are included, with a manual that discusses the relevant areas of employment law and the options available to employers and employees. Free CD with contracts and recruitment and management letters, etc., included.

Code P110 | ISBN 1 902646 37 1 | Sealed wallet | 307 x 217 mm | £9.99 | 1st Edition

LAST WILL & TESTAMENT

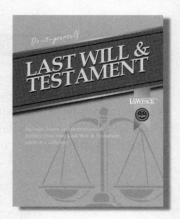

With the help of this Guide, writing a Will can be a straightforward matter. It takes the reader step by step through the process of drawing up a Will, while providing background information and advice. Will forms, completed examples and checklists are included. Covers executors and guardians, making your bequests, property that does not pass under your Will, gifts and substitutional beneficiaries, safe-keeping of a Will.

Code B403 | ISBN 1 902646 85 1 | PB | 246 x189mm | 80pp | £9.99 | 3rd Edition

PROBATE

What happens when someone dies, with or without leaving a Will, and their estate needs to be dealt with? Probate is the process by which the deceased's executors apply for authority to handle the deceased's assets. This Guide provides the information and easy-to-follow instructions needed to obtain a grant of probate, or grant of letters of administration, and administer an estate without the expense of a solicitor.

Code B409 | ISBN 1 902646 27 4 | PB | 246 x 189mm | 112pp | £9.99 | 2nd edition

POWERS OF ATTORNEY & LIVING WILL

You never know when you might need someone to act on your behalf with full legal authority. What if you became seriously ill and needed your business and personal interests looked after? This Guide explains the difference between an Enduring Power of Attorney and a General Power of Attorney and shows how to create both. With the Living Will in this Guide, you can also express your wishes regarding future medical treatment.

Code B410 | ISBN 1 902646 69 X | PB | 246 x 189mm | 96pp | £9.99 | 3rd Edition

HOUSE BUYING SELLING & CONVEYANCING

It isn't true that only those who have gone through long, expensive and involved training can possibly understand the intricacies of house buying, selling and conveyancing. This Guide is a new, updated edition of a best-selling book by Joseph Bradshaw, once described in The Times as the 'guru of layperson conveyancing', which explains just how straightforward the whole process really is. Required reading for all house buyers (or sellers).

Code B412 | ISBN 1 902646 70 3 | PB | 246 x 189mm | 192pp | £9.99 | 2nd Edition

RENT BOOK

The Law Pack 'all-in-one' Rent Book has been specially prepared for use with all the commonly occurring types of letting: assured and assured shorthold tenancies, restricted contract lettings, and protected or statutory tenancies. It includes the notices and information for tenants that are required by law for each type of letting. A rent book or similar document is required in those tenancy situations where rent is paid on a weekly basis.

Code RB001 | ISBN 1 902646 63 0 | PB | 170 x 100mm | 16pp | £1.59 inc.VAT | 1st Edition

RESIDENTIAL LETTINGS

This Guide is required reading for anyone letting residential property. It provides all that a would-be landlord needs to know before letting a flat or house. It covers the legal background, preparation of the property, finding a tenant, the tenancy agreement, problem tenants, buy-to-let, HMOs and more.
'Residential Lettings *amounts to a management tool no landlord should be without'*, National Federation of Residential Landlords

Code B422 | ISBN 1 904053 01 7 | PB | 246 x 189mm | 120pp | £9.99 | 2nd Edition

EMPLOYMENT LAW

Whether you are an employer or an employee, you have rights in the workplace. This best-selling Guide, by employment law solicitor Melanie Hunt, is a comprehensive source of knowledge on hiring, wages, employment contracts, family-friendly rights, discrimination, termination and other important issues. It puts at your fingertips all the important legal points employers and employees should know about.

Code B408 | ISBN 1 902646 98 3 | PB | 246 x 189mm | 160pp | £9.99 | 5th Edition

LIMITED COMPANY

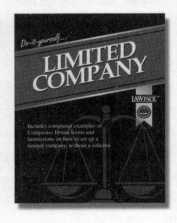

Do you want to set up a business? This Guide explains what a limited company is and how it is structured and describes how to set one up yourself and save on legal fees. It explains the procedures, and includes examples of Companies House forms, Memoranda of Association, Articles of Association and director's resolutions. Valid in England and Wales, and Scotland.

Code B405 | ISBN 1 902646 58 4 | PB | 246 x 189mm | 96pp | £9.99 | 3rd Edition

COMPANY SECRETARY

This book is what every time-pressed company secretary or record-keeper needs. Maintaining good, up-to-date records of company meetings and resolutions is not only good practice but also a legal requirement, whatever size your company is. This book of forms makes compiling minutes of board and shareholder meetings straightforward. It includes more than 125 commonly-required resolutions and minutes: all that a limited company is likely to need.

Code B416 | ISBN 1 902646 19 3 | PB | A4 | 188pp | £19.99 | 2nd Edition

PERSONNEL MANAGER

A book of more than 200 do-it-yourself forms, contracts and letters to help you manage your personnel needs more effectively. As employment laws and codes of practice increasingly affect the workplace, good, efficient record-keeping is essential for any employer, large or small. There's no quicker or easier way to 'get it in writing' than using *Personnel Manager*. Areas covered include recruitment & hiring, employment contracts & agreements, handling new employees, personnel management, performance evaluation and termination of employment.

Code B417 | ISBN 1 902646 02 9 | PB | A4 | 262pp | £19.99 | 2nd Edition

301 LEGAL FORMS, LETTERS & AGREEMENTS

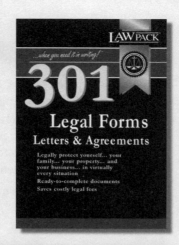

Our best-selling Form Book now in its seventh edition. It is packed with forms, letters and agreements for legal protection in virtually every situation. It provides a complete do-it-yourself library of 301 ready-to-use legal documents, for business or personal use. Areas covered include loans and borrowing, buying and selling, employment, transfers and assignments and residential tenancy.

Code B402 | ISBN 1 902646 72 X | PB | A4 | 358pp | £19.99 | 7th Edition

LEGAL ADVISER

Fast answers to nearly all your legal questions! *Legal Adviser* is a comprehensive and succinct guide on the different ways the law influences our everyday lives. It covers such topics as setting up home, children, tax, employment, buying goods and services, neighbours, sports, holidays, motoring, the police, data protection and inheritance. It is a clear and reliable guide to one's rights under the law and an invaluable reference work. Lists of organisations to turn to for help are also included.

Code B421 | ISBN 1 902646 53 3 | PB | 245 x 199mm | 368pp | £15.99 | 1st edition

PERSONAL INJURY CLAIMS

Many people are not aware of the compensation that may be available to them as a result of injury at work, play, on the road, from a defective product, or through medical negligence. In this topical Guide, barrister Felicity Mileham sets out what losses you may claim for, how to collect evidence, how the court procedure works and what sums of money the courts award. It also provides guidance on what defences are available, should someone be making a claim against you.

Code B424 | ISBN 1 902646 59 2 | PB | 246 x 189mm | 216pp | £9.99 | 1st Edition

SMALL CLAIMS

If you want to take action to recover a debt, resolve a contract dispute or make a personal injury claim, you can file your own small claim without a solicitor. This Guide includes clear instructions and advice on how to handle your own case and enforce judgment.

Code B406 | ISBN 1 902646 04 5 | PB | A4 | 96pp | £9.99 | 2nd Edition

MOTORING LAW

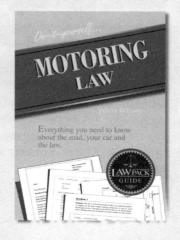

Whether we like it or not, motoring is a fact of everyday life. But how many drivers actually know their rights and those of the police? The Highway Code provides the driving basics. This Guide is essential follow-up reading on the motorist's real rights and remedies.

Code B415 | ISBN 1 898217 51 3 | PB | A4 | 104pp | £9..99 | 1st Edition

DIVORCE

File your own undefended divorce and save legal fees! This Guide explains the process from filing your petition to final decree. Even if there are complications such as young children or contested grounds this Guide will save you time and money.

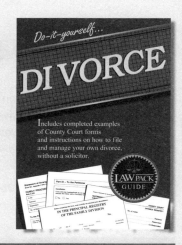

Code B404 | ISBN 1 902646 05 3 | PB | A4 | 120pp | £9.99 | 2nd Edition

COHABITATION RIGHTS

As more couples choose not to marry, the legal and financial issues they face with parental responsibility, mortgages, separation and death become ever more important to understand and address. This book by Philippa Pearson, a partner at a leading firm of family law lawyers, mediators and counsellors, discusses the options in cohabitation agreements, which cover financial matters, and non-legal 'living together' agreements, and provides practical advice for couples.

Code B423 | ISBN 1 902646 52 5 | PB | 246 x 189mm | 104pp | £9.99 | 1st Edition

HOME & FAMILY SOLICITOR

The essential do-it-yourself legal resource for every home. From taking action against a noisy neighbour to drawing up a live-in nanny's employment contract, this book of forms will provide you with the ideal, ready-to-use legal letter or agreement. Covers: credit and finance, employment, goods, services and utilities, insurance, personal and family matters, lettings and property, and local environment.

Code B418 | ISBN 1 902646 30 4 | PB | A4 | 232 | £19.99 | 3rd Edition

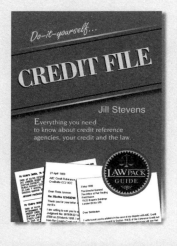

CREDIT FILE

Refused credit? Bad credit? We nearly all rely on credit, whether it be with the bank, mortgage lender or credit card company. This Guide explains just how credit agencies work, what goes on to your credit file and what legitimate action you can take to improve it. It divulges lenders' decision-making processes and blows the lid off 'credit repair' and credit 'blacklists'.

Code B413 | ISBN 1 898217 77 7 | PB | A4 | 96pp | £9.99 | 1st Edition

LEGAL ADVICE HANDBOOK

Where do you go for legal advice? As the sources of free and paid-for legal advice become more diverse and different areas of law demand greater specialisation from the advice givers, the need for a consumer guide to this unmapped network has never been greater. Solicitor Tessa Shepperson has researched the whole field of offline and online advice and has produced an invaluable handbook.

Code B427 | ISBN 1 902646 71 1 | PB | A5 | 192pp | £7.99 | 1st Edition

HOW TO COMPLAIN EFFECTIVELY

Faulty goods, shoddy service, poor advice... these are things most of us, at some time, feel we have good reason to complain about. In this practical guide, Steve Wiseman draws on his extensive experience as a Citizens Advice Bureau manager and tells you how to ensure your complaint has maximum impact, whether it be against your local shop or a government department.

Code B430 | ISBN 1 902646 80 0 | PB | A5 | 160pp | £7.99 | 1st Edition

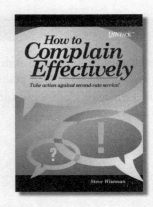

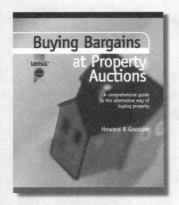

BUYING BARGAINS AT PROPERTY AUCTIONS

Every week, hundreds of commercial and residential properties are sold at auction in Britain, often at bargain prices, with owner-occupiers accounting for a growing proportion of buyers. In this best-selling guide, author and property auctioneer Howard Gooddie spells out how straightforward the auction route can be and divulges the tips and practices of this relatively unknown world.

Code B426 | ISBN 1 902646 68 1 | PB | 245 x 199mm | 168pp | £11.99 | 1st Edition

TAX ANSWERS AT A GLANCE

With tax self-assessment, we all need to have a hold of the panoply of taxes now levied by government. Compiled by tax experts and presented in question-and-answer format, this handy guide provides a useful and digestible summary of income tax, VAT, capital gains, inheritance, pensions, self-employment, partnerships, land and property, trusts and estates, corporation tax, stamp duty and more.

Code B425 | ISBN 1 902646 62 2 | PB | A5 | 176pp | £7.99 | 1st Edition

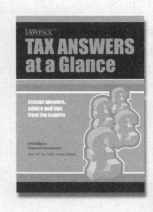

THE LEGAL GUIDE TO ONLINE BUSINESS

Going online opens up a world of legal issues that can't be ignored. Domain names, trade marks, international jurisdictions, credit card transactions, partnerships, alliances, online contracts, employee email and internet policies and cyber crimes are some of the issues discussed and explained by specialist solicitor, Susan Singleton. Template documents included.

Code B603 | ISBN 1 902646 77 0 | 250 x 199 mm | 168pp | £9.99 | 1st Edition

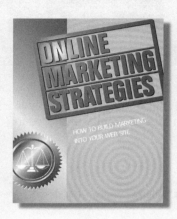

ONLINE MARKETING STRATEGIES

What are your goals for your web site? Is your web site marketing you, or are you marketing it? And how will your web site relate to your business's overall marketing strategy? This book provides guidance on building marketing into your web site, on monitoring, evaluating and improving your internet or extranet site and on coordinating online and offline marketing strategies.

Code B602 | ISBN 1 902646 75 4 | 250 x 199 mm | 160pp | £9.99 | 1st Edition

SECRETS OF SUCCESSFUL WEB SITES

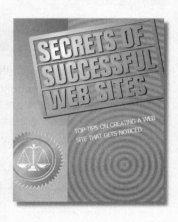

Some web sites get it right, many get it wrong. This guide divulges what makes a successful site. It covers identifying the audience and their needs, choosing the right model for your site, choosing the right technology and ISP, getting the best help with implementation, design and branding, risk management and testing procedures.

Code B601 | ISBN 1 902646 74 6 | 250 x 199 mm | 112pp | £9.99 | 1st Edition

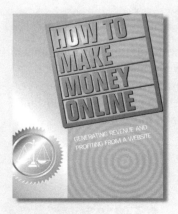

HOW TO MAKE MONEY ONLINE

Forget the high-profile dot com failures - there are businesses out there making money online. This guide includes what will and won't sell, how to avoid e-business mistakes, how to give web site visitors the confidence to buy online, getting payments, security software and systems, digital certificates and e-signatures, selling advertising space, supplying content, and much more!

Code B604 | ISBN 1 902646 76 2 | 250 x 199 mm | 96pp | £9.99 | 1st Edition

BUSINESS LETTERS I & BUSINESS LETTERS II

Business Letters I and Business Letters II are complementary Made Easy Guides, each providing an invaluable source of more than 100 ready-drafted, annotated letters to take away the headache and time-wasting of letter writing. Business Letters I covers managing suppliers, managing customers, debt collection and credit control. Business Letters II covers employing people, sales and marketing management, banking insurance and property, business and the community and international trade.

| Business Letters I Code B504 | ISBN 1 902646 38 X | PB | 250 x 199mm | 160pp | £9.99 | 1st Edition |
| Business Letters II Code B505 | ISBN 1 902646 39 8 | PB | 250 x 199mm | 168pp | £9.99 | 1st Edition |

RUNNING YOUR OWN BUSINESS

You have a business idea that you want to put into action, but you also want advice on the realities of setting up and running a business: this Made Easy Guide is for you. It takes you through the business-creation process, from assessing your aptitude and ideas, to funding and business plans.

| Code B511 | ISBN 1 902646 47 9 | PB | 250 x 199mm | 146pp | £9.99 | 1st Edition |

COMPANY MINUTES & RESOLUTIONS

Company Minutes & Resolutions Made Easy is what every busy company secretary or record-keeper needs. Maintaining good, up-to-date records is not only sensible business practice, but also a legal requirement of Companies House. This Made Easy Guide makes the whole process straightforward. It provides an invaluable source of essential documents that no company should be without.

| Code B501 | ISBN 1 902646 41 X | PB | 250 x 199mm | 198pp | £9.99 | 1st Edition |

DEBT COLLECTION

Chasing debts is a pain which all businesses can do without. Unfortunately, unpaid bills are an all-too frequent problem for business owners and managers. *Debt Collection Made Easy* helps you solve it. It provides expert advice and tips on resolving disputes, reducing the risks of bad debt, getting money out of reluctant payers, letter cycles, credit insurance, export credit, and much more.

| Code B512 | ISBN 1 902646 42 8 | PB | 250 x 199mm | 144pp | £9.99 | 1st Edition |

STRESS MANAGEMENT

Stress can be harmful, negative and costly - a barrier to efficiency and a drain on personal, physical and financial resources. This book provides a blueprint for stress management. It covers common stressors, stress auditing, role conflicts and assertiveness, improving working relationships, changing organisational culture and climate, and helping employees with individual assistance programmes.

| Code B429 | ISBN 1 902646 79 7 | PB | 250 x 199mm | 168pp | £9.99 | 1st Edition |